S0-BCQ-696

Merry Christmas
to My "Awesome" Son Jack,
Happy Reading
Forever!

Love Mommy

:)

Don't Be Afraid of Anything Ever

—— " ——

-2013-

Dragons

and Other Mythical

Monsters

Fearsome Creatures from Myth and Fiction

Dragons

and Other Mythical

Monsters

Fearsome Creatures from Myth and Fiction

GENERAL EDITOR:
GERRIE McCALL AND CHRIS McNAB

amber
BOOKS

Reprinted in 2013

ISBN 978-1-78274-071-1

Editorial and design by
Amber Books Ltd
74–77 White Lion Street
London N1 9PF
United Kingdom
Website: www.amberbooks.co.uk
Appstore: itunes.com/apps/amberbooksltd
Facebook: www.facebook.com/amberbooks
Twitter: @amberbooks
Email: enquiries@amberbooks.co.uk

Project Editor: Sarah Uttridge
Design: Keren Harragan, Andrew Easton and Graham Curd

Printed in China

Picture credits:
All illustrations @ Amber Books Ltd (Illustrator Myke Taylor/The Art Agency) except p10-11, 18-21, 28-29, 32-33, 38-41, 46-47, 50-53, 58-61, 68-69, 80-95 © IMP AB

Contents

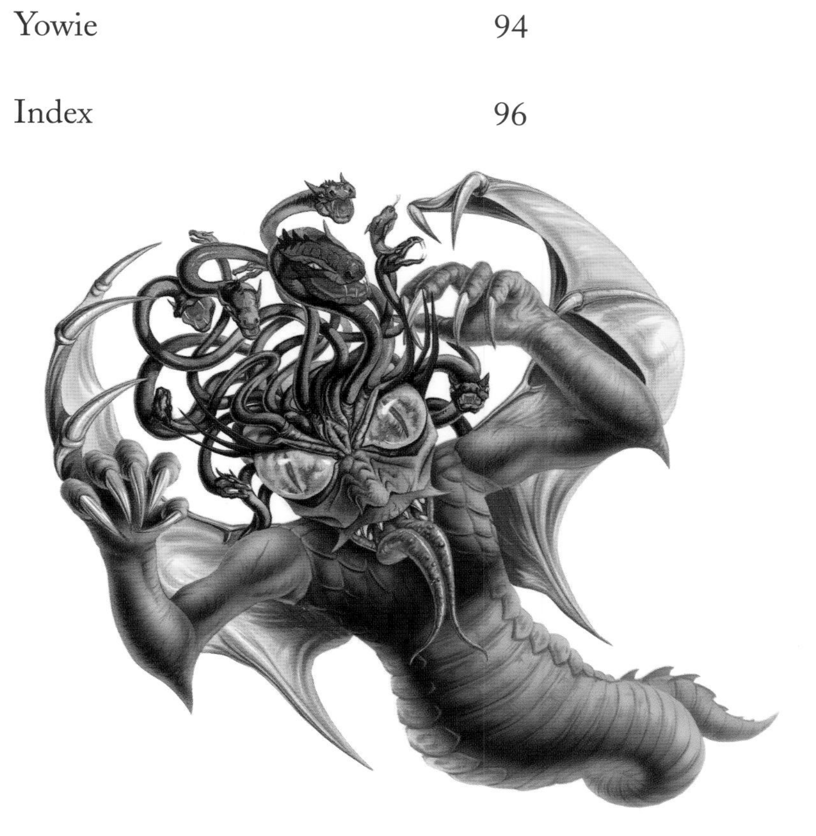

Introduction

For as long as humans have had fears, there have been stories about monsters. Some monsters were born of literature and myth—creatures such as Cyclops, the Sphinx, and the Minotaur. For ancient people, these were not mere fantasies, but real beliefs that haunted their lives. The citizens of Ancient Greece, for example, believed they faced an afterlife meeting with the three-headed dog Cerberus. In North America, Native Americans would tremble in fear of the Thunderbird every time a storm slashed through the sky.

Legends of many ancient monsters survived to terrorize people born hundreds of years later. The Basilisk, a lethal hybrid creature first described 2,000 years ago by the Roman writer Pliny, was still feared and encountered by the 16th century AD. In 1587, a Basilisk was said to have killed two young girls who were hiding in their cellar in Poland.

But haven't we moved on since then? Don't we know now that monsters are just products of fantasy? Don't be so sure. Several of the monsters in this book are certainly figures of pure invention. King Kong was created for cinema in 1933, and Godzilla has been a star of film and print for more than 50 years. Yet, countless witnesses throughout history have claimed that monsters are every bit as real as you or me—they have seen them with their own eyes! Thousands of people, for example, say they have seen the Loch Ness Monster. Scientists still aren't able to explain the sightings and huge footprints of Bigfoot. Reports of Reptoid aliens come from around the world. And more than 1,000 people claimed to witness the Jersey Devil in 1909.

All monster stories lurk somewhere between fantasy and reality. Everyone knows that some creatures are pure myth, but people love to hear a good story! Oftentimes, skeptics discredit modern monster stories by giving scientific explanations—like Bigfoot is just a big ape. But what's so wrong with believing? Thousands of witnesses can't all be lying, right? Don't let the skeptics fool you. It's human nature to be interested in the unknown, and many people—even the nonbelievers—secretly want to believe in these strange beasts.

Beowulf's Dragon

WINGS
Batlike wings attached to the torso by robust muscles lift the dragon in flight. The bones within the wing structure are hollow to reduce their weight.

TAIL
The barbed tail shaped like an arrowhead can be used as a weapon in battle. In flight, the tail operates like a rudder, balancing the dragon and allowing it to execute skillful aerial maneuvers.

EYES
Adapted to see in the dim light of caves, the dragon's eyes are well suited for watching over its hoard of plundered treasure.

JAWS
Its fiery breath lights the skies. Chain mail provides no defense against its crushing jaws and poisonous fangs. A reservoir of venom is located in the upper jaw.

BODY
The dragon's enormous body is blackened by the soot of its own flames. Its blue-green scales glow with inner fire.

Coiled in a cavern beneath a gray rock there is a terrifying dragon—a fire drake measuring 50 ft. (15 m) long. The dragon guards a lair filled with piles of priceless treasure. Its heavy body blocks daylight from reaching the armor, goblets, jewels, coins, and golden swords it hoards deep in the cave. When a thief steals a golden cup from its lair, the dragon rampages through the countryside, burning everything it sees. The fire drake breathes flames that light up the sky, terrifying villagers and burning every home in Geatland. Beowulf, King of the Geats, armed with a magic sword, leads an army into battle to face the dragon.

ACTUAL SIZE

▶ BEOWULF STRIKES THE DRAGON WITH HIS SWORD, but the blow glances off the beast's terrible hide. Beowulf is engulfed in dragon flames, a sight so terrifying that his army flees. Only the faithful Wiglaf remains to help. Beowulf breaks off the blade of his magic sword in the dragon's head. Bitten on the neck by the dragon, Beowulf is soaked in his own blood but continues fighting. Wiglaf stabs the dragon in a vulnerable place and Beowulf slashes it through the middle, cutting the monster in two and ending its life.

Where in the world?

Geatland, a region in the south of Sweden, is where Beowulf met the mighty dragon in battle. Geatland's deep forests provided the ideal habitat for a fire drake.

Did you know?

- Beowulf dies from his battle wounds. The dragon's treasure is removed from the cave and buried with Beowulf. All the pieces of the dragon's corpse are thrown into the sea.
- The dragon's flames are so intense that they burn Wiglaf's shield down to its handle. Wooden shields, such as the one Wiglaf used, are a poor choice when doing battle with a fire drake.
- Beowulf carries an iron shield bearing the image of a dragon.
- A dragon's lightweight bones are tougher than reinforced concrete.
- Smoke rising from the mouth of a cave is usually a telltale sign that a dragon resides within.
- The dragon is the largest-known flying creature.

Chupacabra

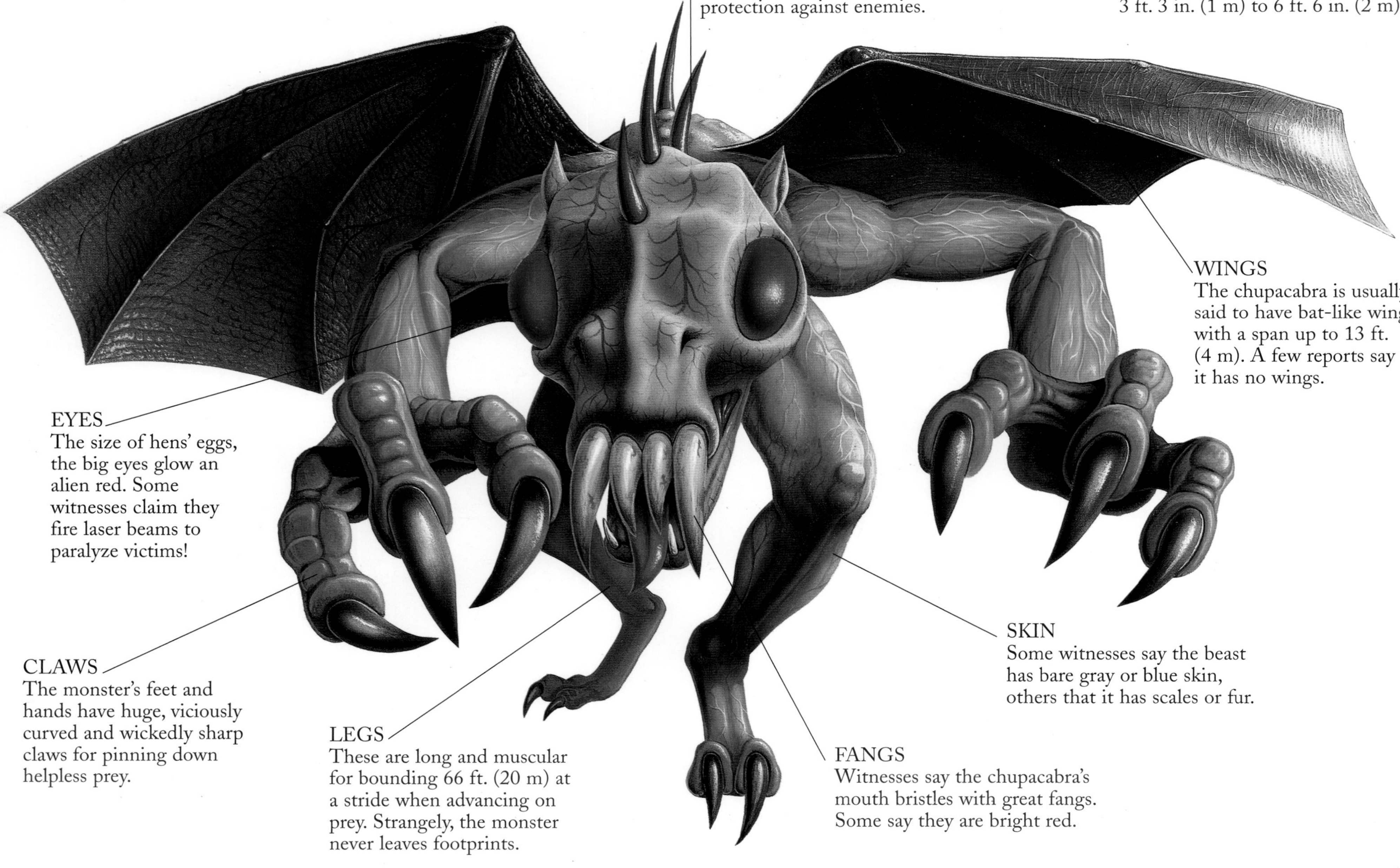

SPINES
These reportedly burst through the skin of the monster's head and back. Their purpose is unknown, but they may offer protection against enemies.

SIZE
Eyewitness accounts are muddled. Estimates of the creature's height in the standing position vary from 3 ft. 3 in. (1 m) to 6 ft. 6 in. (2 m).

WINGS
The chupacabra is usually said to have bat-like wings with a span up to 13 ft. (4 m). A few reports say it has no wings.

EYES
The size of hens' eggs, the big eyes glow an alien red. Some witnesses claim they fire laser beams to paralyze victims!

SKIN
Some witnesses say the beast has bare gray or blue skin, others that it has scales or fur.

CLAWS
The monster's feet and hands have huge, viciously curved and wickedly sharp claws for pinning down helpless prey.

LEGS
These are long and muscular for bounding 66 ft. (20 m) at a stride when advancing on prey. Strangely, the monster never leaves footprints.

FANGS
Witnesses say the chupacabra's mouth bristles with great fangs. Some say they are bright red.

A modern menace of the Americas, this bloodsucking, bat-like fiend is blamed by farmers and the authorities alike for the brutal slaughter of pets and livestock. This multi-fanged, many-spined, foul-smelling monster was first reported in 1995. It seeks out its victims in the dark of night and preys on a range of farm and domestic animals, sucking them dry of blood – its name means "goat-sucker," after its first victim. Some people say that the chupacabra comes from outer space, while others say it is the result of US military experiments.

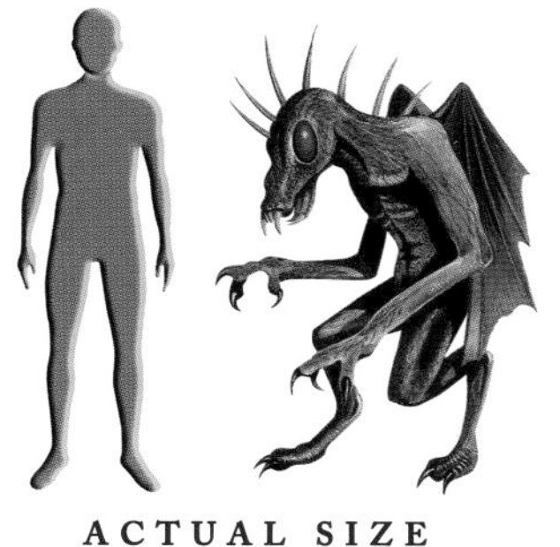

ACTUAL SIZE

A CHUPACABRA SWOOPS TOWARD A SMALL HERD OF GOATS and drops silently between the trees —a ragged silhouette against the night sky. Sensing danger, the goats shuffle nervously, then start to bleat in panic as the monster strides toward them, moving unnaturally fast on its long legs. Paralyzed by terror and the foul, sulfurous odor of the chupacabra, the goats are helpless to flee. The monster seizes the nearest one with its claws, plunges its huge fangs into the animal, and swiftly sucks out every last drop of blood. Goat after goat, it drains the whole herd, then slips off in search of other prey—for a chupacabra's craving for blood is never satisfied. It leaves no tracks behind.

Where in the world?

The chupacabra is known in Central and South America. There are also reports from the southern states of the USA, including California, Arizona, Texas and Florida. Most sightings are from Puerto Rico, an island 994 miles (1600km) southeast of Florida.

Did you know?

- Two Brazilian fishermen claim they shot a chupacabra dead and still have its head—which they refuse to let anyone examine.
- The mayor of Canovanas, a town in Puerto Rico, leads chupacabra search parties, armed with a crucifix and a gun. He also sets traps around the town in the hope of catching one of the elusive creatures.
- In 1996, a Mexican policeman opened fire on a chupacabra at close range—but his bullets had no effect, and the monster escaped.
- Attacks on humans are rare, but a nurse in Mexico reportedly lost an arm to the fangs of a chupacabra.

Gorynych

BODY
The scaly body produces a reek of sulfur that hangs around Gorynych like a sinister cloud.
HEADS
Three fanged, fire-spitting heads with terrible horns make it impossible to approach Gorynych. Six watchful eyes and a heightened sense of smell enable him to detect a maiden from a mile (1.6 km) away.
CLAWS
Iron claws rip knights' suits of armor open as if they were aluminum cans.
WINGS
Although his great bulk prevents him from flying quickly, Gorynych's wings allow him to descend in places where he is least expected.
TAILS
Seven wildly thrashing tails render the dragon's back end as hazardous as his front.

This savage Russian dragon has three fire-spitting heads and seven tails. Gorynych walks on his two hind legs and has two small front legs, like a Tyrannosaurus rex. His iron claws can slash through any shield or suit of armor. The air around Gorynych reeks of sulfur, a sign of its evil. His uncle, the sorcerer Nemal Chelovek, kidnaps the czar's daughter and intends her to wed Gorynych. The princess is imprisoned in the sorcerer's dark mountain castle. Desperate to have his daughter back, the czar offers a huge reward to anyone who can rescue the princess from the castle. Many princes try and fail.

ACTUAL SIZE

▶ IVAN, A PALACE GUARD who understands the speech of animals, overhears two crows discussing where the princess is hidden. The czar gives Ivan a magic sword to help him on his rescue mission. Nemal Chelovek's fortress is unguarded because he believes no one would dare approach him. Nemal Chelovek turns himself into a giant when he discovers Ivan in his castle. The magic sword flies from Ivan's hands, killing the giant, then flies through the castle halls until it finds and slays Gorynych. Ivan marries the princess.

Where in the world?

The fearsome seven-tailed Gorynych is featured in folktales and myths originating from Russia and Ukraine.

Did you know?

- Gorynych caused eclipses of the Sun and Moon. The fact that they reappeared showed that even a powerful dragon could not defeat the Sun and Moon. The Russians took this as a sign that dragons can be defeated by the righteous.

- Not all Slavic dragons are destructive. The Slovenian city of Ljubljana is protected by a dragon. This benevolent dragon is pictured on the city's coat of arms.

- Dragon blood is so venomous that Earth does not absorb it.

- There are no cave paintings of dragons because caves are a favorite residence of dragons. The dragon residing in the cave would have driven all cave painters away.

- A magic sword that enables the warrior to stand far away from the dragon is the ideal weapon for battle with dragons.

Knucker

EYES
Eerie eyes glow with a chemical that allows the Knucker to see great distances in the densest waters and on land.

TAIL
Capable of swatting down trees, the gigantic tail is the dragon's most dangerous appendage.

WINGS
Small wings allow the Knucker to fly low through marshy areas in search of likely victims. When in water, the wings act as fins.

JAWS
Immense jaws open wide enough to swallow a horse and cart whole. Teeth larger than railroad spikes line a mouth that reeks of the Knucker's nauseating breath.

BODY
A streamlined, eel-shaped body aids the Knucker in navigating quickly and silently through the chilly waters of the knuckerhole.

A terrible, water-dwelling dragon, the Knucker makes nightly raids on Lyminster farms for meals of horses and cows. Any person crossing its path is just another meal to the Knucker. The dragon squeezes its prey to death or shreds its victim's flesh to ribbons with its poisonous fangs. The thrashing of the Knucker's immense tail topples the trees in Batworth Park. Many a still night in Lyminster is shattered by the hiss and roar of the ravenous dragon. So many villagers and farm animals go missing that the mayor offers a reward to anyone who can kill the Knucker and allow the villagers to live without fear.

ACTUAL SIZE

▶ JIM, A FARMER'S BOY FROM A NEARBY VILLAGE, tells the mayor his plan to defeat the Knucker. The mayor orders the villagers to help Jim with everything he needs. The villagers give Jim all the ingredients for an enormous pie. Jim bakes a gigantic pie laced with poison for the Knucker. He hauls the pie out to the knuckerhole using a borrowed cart and horse. The Knucker eats the pie, horse, and cart. The poison kills the dreaded dragon and Jim chops off its head with an ax.

Where in the world?

The Knucker rises from the knuckerhole in Lyminster, West Sussex. Its residence, the knuckerhole, is a bottomless pool fed by an underground spring.

Did you know?

- St. Mary Magdalene Church in Lyminster contains the Slayer's Slab, a gravestone dedicated to the hero who killed the Knucker.
- The British explorer Sir Francis Drake was called "The Dragon" by the Spanish because he was a fierce warrior and he helped defeat the Spanish Armada.
- The knuckerhole where the Knucker lives is a bottomless pool that neither freezes in winter nor dries up in summer. Six bell ropes from Lyminster Church were tied together and let down in the knuckerhole to measure its depth, but the bottom was never found.
- Residents of Lyminster once used water from the knuckerhole as a cure-all tonic.
- The county of Sussex once had a thriving dragon population. Bignor Hill and St. Leonard's Forest in Sussex also have a history of dragon infestations.

Krak's Dragon

In Polish legend, a fearsome dragon lives in a dark cave at the foot of Wawel Hill along the banks of the Vistula River. Every day it rages through the countryside, terrifying the inhabitants of Krakow. The bad-tempered, fire-breathing dragon eats farm animals and people. Anything that runs from it is fair game. After it gobbles down several small children, it plunders homes for prized possessions to take back to its cave. Many bold knights try to slay this dragon and perish in flame for their efforts. Its daily thefts begin to affect the local economy. The people of the area grow poorer and the princess worries she will never marry.

ACTUAL SIZE

▶ KRAK, A PEASANT BOY employed as a shoemaker's apprentice, is intelligent, cunning, and possessed of unique culinary skills. The king is desperate for anyone's dragon-slaying services and allows the raggedly dressed boy to try. Krak stuffs three roasted sheep full of sulfur and hot spices and leaves the spicy meal next to the dragon's cave. The greedy dragon gulps them down whole. The spices and sulfur burn the dragon's stomach. It drinks half the Vistula River to quench its thirst. Its swollen, burning gut bursts and kills it.

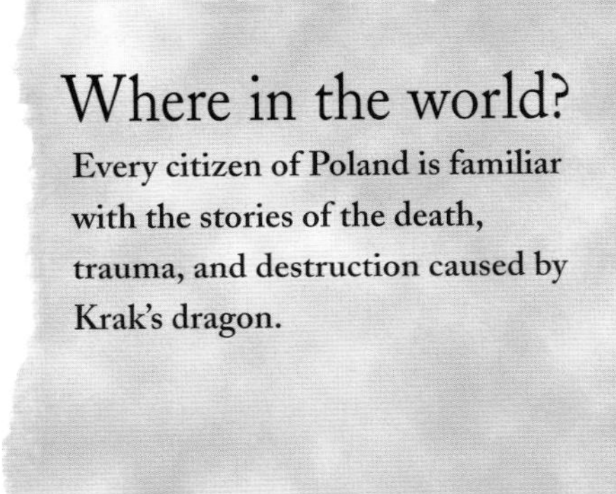

Where in the world?

Every citizen of Poland is familiar with the stories of the death, trauma, and destruction caused by Krak's dragon.

Did you know?

- The city of Krakow is named after the heroic Krak.
- Near the cavern beneath the castle of Krakow, there is a monument to Krak's dragon. The statue of the dragon has been rigged with a natural gas nozzle so that it breathes fire every few minutes.
- Krak marries the princess and is given the dragon's hoarded treasure. After the death of the king, Krak ascends the throne.
- Many dragons prefer to sleep on top of a pile of jewels and treasure because more traditional bedding materials are too easily ignited by their fiery breath.
- Trickery is often the preferred method for defeating the most dangerous dragons. Cunning is generally a mightier weapon than a sword when facing a beast of such tremendous size, aggression, and appetite.

Leviathan

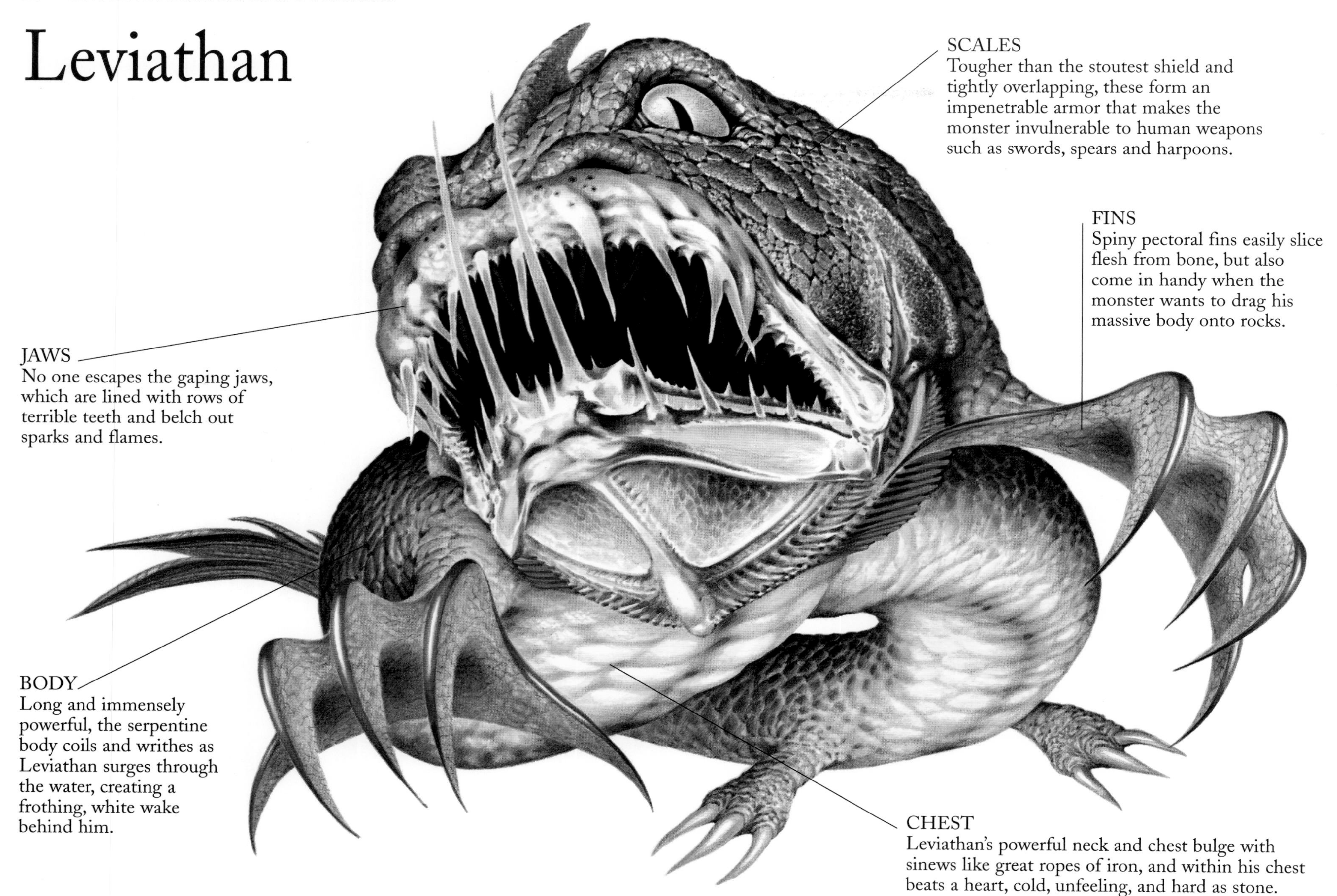
SCALES
Tougher than the stoutest shield and tightly overlapping, these form an impenetrable armor that makes the monster invulnerable to human weapons such as swords, spears and harpoons.
FINS
Spiny pectoral fins easily slice flesh from bone, but also come in handy when the monster wants to drag his massive body onto rocks.
JAWS
No one escapes the gaping jaws, which are lined with rows of terrible teeth and belch out sparks and flames.
BODY
Long and immensely powerful, the serpentine body coils and writhes as Leviathan surges through the water, creating a frothing, white wake behind him.
CHEST
Leviathan's powerful neck and chest bulge with sinews like great ropes of iron, and within his chest beats a heart, cold, unfeeling, and hard as stone.

This primeval sea monster dominates the watery wastes of the world and has power over all the creatures of the ocean. He is chaos and evil personified, and he brings death and disaster in his foaming wake. His body stinks like a rotten carcass and he drinks the entire flow of rivers every day. His furnace-hot breath makes the sea boil, and when he sneezes, smoke billows from his nose. The Leviathan is first mentioned in Middle Eastern creation myths dating back more than 5000 years. According to Hebrew texts, Yahweh (God) made Leviathan and a female mate on the fifth day of Creation, but promptly killed the female to stop her producing offspring that might destabilize the world.

ACTUAL SIZE

▶ STIRRING UP THE OCEAN WITH HIS MIGHTY TAIL, Leviathan creates a seething wall of water that gathers speed, bursts over the shore and completely overwhelms a small fishing village. Huts are shattered like matchwood and screaming victims are swept out to their deaths. A few locals escape the carnage by climbing trees, and they can only watch in horror as the monster rears out of the water to gloat at his handiwork and gobble up anyone washed out to sea.

Where in the world?

Leviathan has his origins in early Hebrew writings from the Middle East, dating back to about 3000 years BC. The Hebrews occupied Turkey, Syria, Jordan, Israel, Iraq and Iran—but the monster has the run of all the world's oceans.

Did you know?

- Early images of Leviathan from seal-stones and weapons show the monster with seven heads.
- Christians have identified Leviathan with Satan, with his huge mouth being the entrance to Hell.
- Most fish swim willingly into Leviathan's jaws, apart from the tiny stickleback. The Leviathan fears the stickleback because it was created to keep him in check.

Mummy

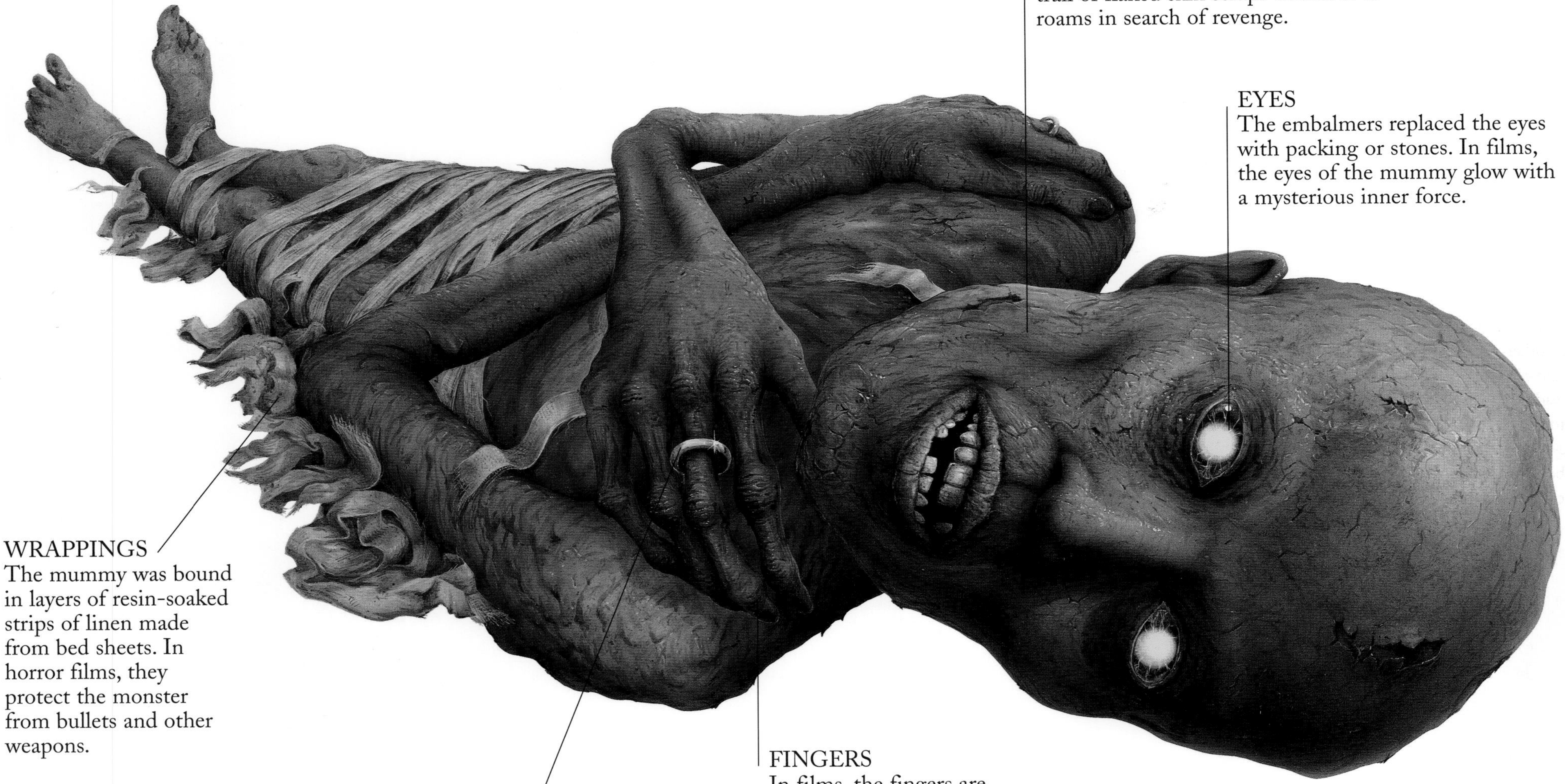

SKIN & LIPS
Embalming dried out the body completely, leaving skin, lips and other tissues cracked and shriveled. In films, the mummy leaves a gruesome trail of flaked skin scraps wherever it roams in search of revenge.

EYES
The embalmers replaced the eyes with packing or stones. In films, the eyes of the mummy glow with a mysterious inner force.

WRAPPINGS
The mummy was bound in layers of resin-soaked strips of linen made from bed sheets. In horror films, they protect the monster from bullets and other weapons.

MAGIC CHARMS
Charms, such as magic rings, gave the mummy great power.

FINGERS
In films, the fingers are long and powerful—ideal for throttling.

Ancient Egyptians carved grim threats on the tombs of their embalmed kings, warning the living not to disturb the grave—or risk the wrath of the mummy. The mummy is an embalmed body that has survived intact in its secret tomb for thousands of years.

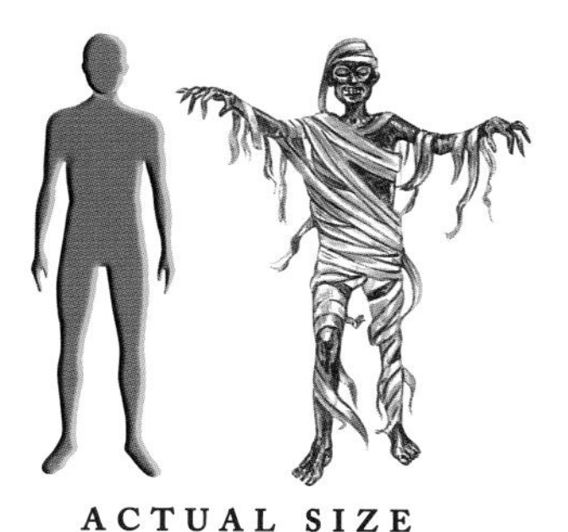
ACTUAL SIZE

Wrapped in strips of linen and sealed away with gold, jewels, and other treasure, it is protected by a curse. In horror films, the mummy comes to life to take revenge on robbers and archaeologists who dare to invade its tomb.

▶ TWO ARCHAEOLOGISTS AND THEIR HIRED WORKERS have spent weeks hacking at the rocks, and now the tomb's entrance is revealed. Also visible are the symbols spelling out a dire threat. The workers grow restless, but the archaeologists dismiss their fears. Using heavy axes, the workers rain blows on the entrance, which shatters with a deafening crack. Holding his blazing torch high, the lead archaeologist enters the tomb, with his colleague close behind. He looks around in awe as the torch's light glints off precious objects decorated with gold and jewels. A movement catches his eye and he turns to see a massive stone coffin open and a huge mummy appear. The mummy lumbers toward him with outstretched arms. Paralyzed with fear, the archaeologist stands helpless as he feels the mummy's powerful hands grip his throat—and begin to squeeze.

Where in the world?

The best-known tombs of mummies are in the Valley of the Kings in Egypt. The mummy of Tutankhamen still lies in his tomb, near the ancient cities of Thebes and Luxor, close to the Nile River. Other tombs were at Abydos, 93 mi. (150 km) farther downriver.

Did you know?

- In medieval times, physicians often sold real or fake mummy's flesh and wrappings in powder form as a medicine. It was used to treat disorders from acne to ulcers.

- Scientists set up the world's first international mummy tissue bank at Manchester Museum, UK, in the late 1990s. It holds tissue samples taken from mummies housed in museums around the world, for use in medical research.

- The Egyptian priests tried many different ways to protect the royal tombs, including inscribing bloodcurdling curses. They built huge granite doors and secret entrances.

Orochi

TAILS
Eight sinuous tails create strange whistling noises as Orochi thrashes them in anger.
EYES
Eight sets of eyes that are as red as winter cherries keep watch in all directions.
BELLY
Perpetually bloody and inflamed from his kills, the ravenous dragon's belly must always be filled.
BODY
The giant body stretches over eight valleys and eight hills. Orochi's back is covered with moss and trees.

Each year the evil dragon Orochi demands that a Japanese maiden be offered to him in sacrifice. Even the bravest of warriors cannot defeat this vicious, cunning beast. His gigantic body slithers across eight hills and valleys, and his eight hungry heads make him impossible to approach. One day Susanoo, the god of the sea and storms, comes upon two weeping parents. Seven of their daughters have been devoured by Orochi in the past seven years. Now their eighth and only remaining daughter is to be sacrificed to Orochi. Susanoo agrees to slay the dragon if their eighth daughter will be his wife.

ACTUAL SIZE

▶ SUSANOO TRANSFORMS THE MAIDEN into a comb, which he safely hides in his hair. Susanoo arranges eight enormous vats of rice wine in a circle and leaves them out to tempt the dragon. Attracted by the smell of the strong wine, Orochi plunges each of his eight heads into a vat and drinks greedily. The drunken dragon collapses helpless to the ground and Susanoo uses his powerful sword to slice Orochi to pieces. The local river runs red with the blood of the slain menace.

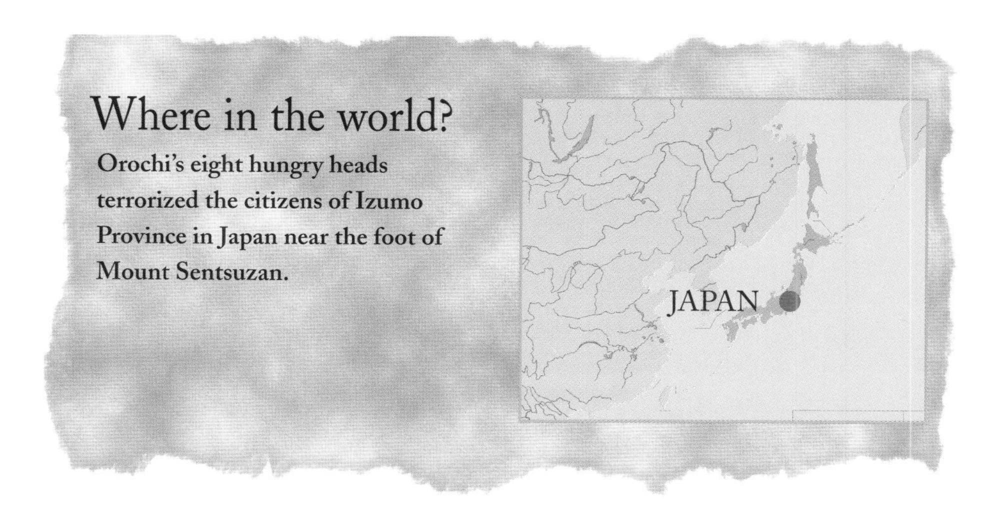

Where in the world?

Orochi's eight hungry heads terrorized the citizens of Izumo Province in Japan near the foot of Mount Sentsuzan.

Did you know?

- As Susanoo hacks up Orochi, he discovers a sacred sword embedded in one of his tails. The screams of the dying dragon could be heard throughout even the furthest islands of Japan.
- The dragon's full name, Yamata no Orochi, means "big snake of eight branches."
- Fresh maidens are a favorite meal of dragons worldwide.
- During the Edo period (1603-1868), it was popular for Japanese firefighters to get dragon tattoos. They believed the image of the dragon would protect them while fighting fires.
- Although fearsome and powerful, Japanese dragons are also fair and benevolent. The Japanese believe dragons bring wealth and good luck.
- Images of dragons adorn many Buddhist temples in Japan. Dragons are thought to dispel evil.

St. George and the Dragon

This bloodthirsty dragon lives by a spring that provides all the water for the city of Cyrene. Whenever the citizens of Cyrene want water, they are faced with the immense beast. Unhappy with the diet of sheep the citizens feed it, the dragon demands human sacrifices. A human sacrifice has to be given to the dragon daily before it allows anyone to draw water from the spring. The only fair way to determine the daily victim is by drawing lots. The princess is chosen as the next victim and her father, the king, is distraught. He offers the citizens all his riches if they will spare his daughter, but the citizens refuse.

ACTUAL SIZE

▶ THE PRINCESS IS TIED TO A WOODEN STAKE near the spring. St. George, a soldier of the Roman Empire, discovers the distressed princess and unties her. St. George charges the dragon on horseback. His sturdy lance penetrates deep enough only to wound the foul creature. Using the princess's sash as a leash, St. George and the princess lead the injured dragon into town. St. George announces he will finish off the dragon if the citizens convert to Christianity. They agree to convert and St. George draws his sword and kills the dragon.

Where in the world?

This dragon nests at a spring that provides water for the citizens of Cyrene, Libya, which is situated in northern Africa.

Did you know?

- St. George is the patron saint of England, knights, archers, and butchers.
- The flag of Wales bears the image of a red dragon. It is believed to be the oldest national flag still in use.
- Hundreds of years ago, dinosaur fossils were believed to be dragon bones.
- Dragoon soldiers carried a musket, called the dragon. The musket was given this name because it emitted flames when fired.
- The various parts of the dragon are believed to have magical properties. Anyone eating dragon's heart would be able to understand the speech of birds. Eating dragon's tongue gives one the power to win any argument. Dragon's blood provides protection against injury from swords.

Wyvern

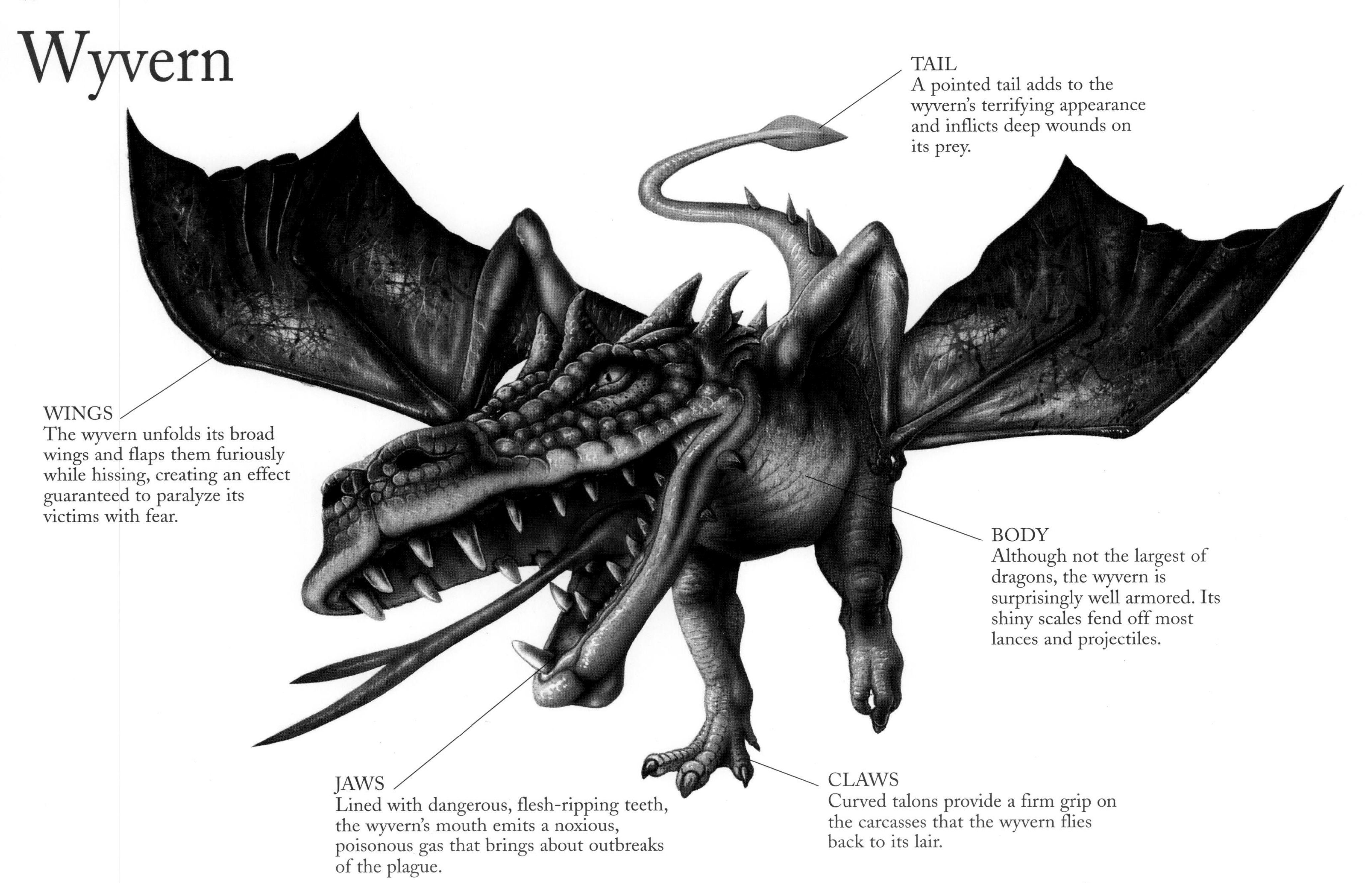
TAIL
A pointed tail adds to the wyvern's terrifying appearance and inflicts deep wounds on its prey.
WINGS
The wyvern unfolds its broad wings and flaps them furiously while hissing, creating an effect guaranteed to paralyze its victims with fear.
BODY
Although not the largest of dragons, the wyvern is surprisingly well armored. Its shiny scales fend off most lances and projectiles.
JAWS
Lined with dangerous, flesh-ripping teeth, the wyvern's mouth emits a noxious, poisonous gas that brings about outbreaks of the plague.
CLAWS
Curved talons provide a firm grip on the carcasses that the wyvern flies back to its lair.

The most famous wyvern is one adopted as a pet by young Maud. While walking in the woods near her home in Mordiford, Maud discovers a baby wyvern. Its body is no bigger than a cucumber and is covered in sparkling, bright-green scales. Maud takes the helpless wyvern home, but her parents forbid her to keep it. Instead of setting it free, Maud places the tiny dragon in her secret hiding place in the woods. She visits it daily, feeding it milk and playing with it. The wyvern grows rapidly and soon milk is not enough to satisfy its ravenous appetite. The wyvern begins to feast on local livestock.

ACTUAL SIZE

▶ THE WYVERN QUICKLY DISCOVERS that farmers make better meals than farm animals. Despite its newly acquired taste for human flesh, the wyvern remains gentle with Maud. Garston, a man from one of Mordiford's best families, dons his armor and rides out to slay the wyvern. His sturdy shield protects Garston from the flame-spouting wyvern. Garston pierces the wyvern's shiny scales with his sword, fatally wounding the creature. Maud kneels on the bloodied grass beside the wyvern. Weeping, she cradles her dying friend in her arms.

Where in the world?

In medieval Mordiford, Herefordshire, in England, wyverns were plentiful. It seemed almost anyone could stumble across one with little effort.

Did you know?

- Because of their flesh-eating habits, wyverns make unsatisfactory pets. Although they are harmless as babies, a dragon's bloodthirsty instincts always set in when it reaches adulthood.
- The wyvern is associated with war, pestilence, and envy. It is believed to bring outbreaks of the plague wherever it goes.
- Its traits of strength, power, and endurance made the wyvern a popular symbol on medieval coats of arms. Its image on shields was used to strike fear into the hearts of enemies.
- British dragons have been known to inhabit places as diverse as caves, fields, woods, swamps, gullies, moors, corn stacks, water holes, and abbey ruins.
- The coat of arms of Moscow bears the image of a soldier on horseback spearing a wyvern.

Basilisk

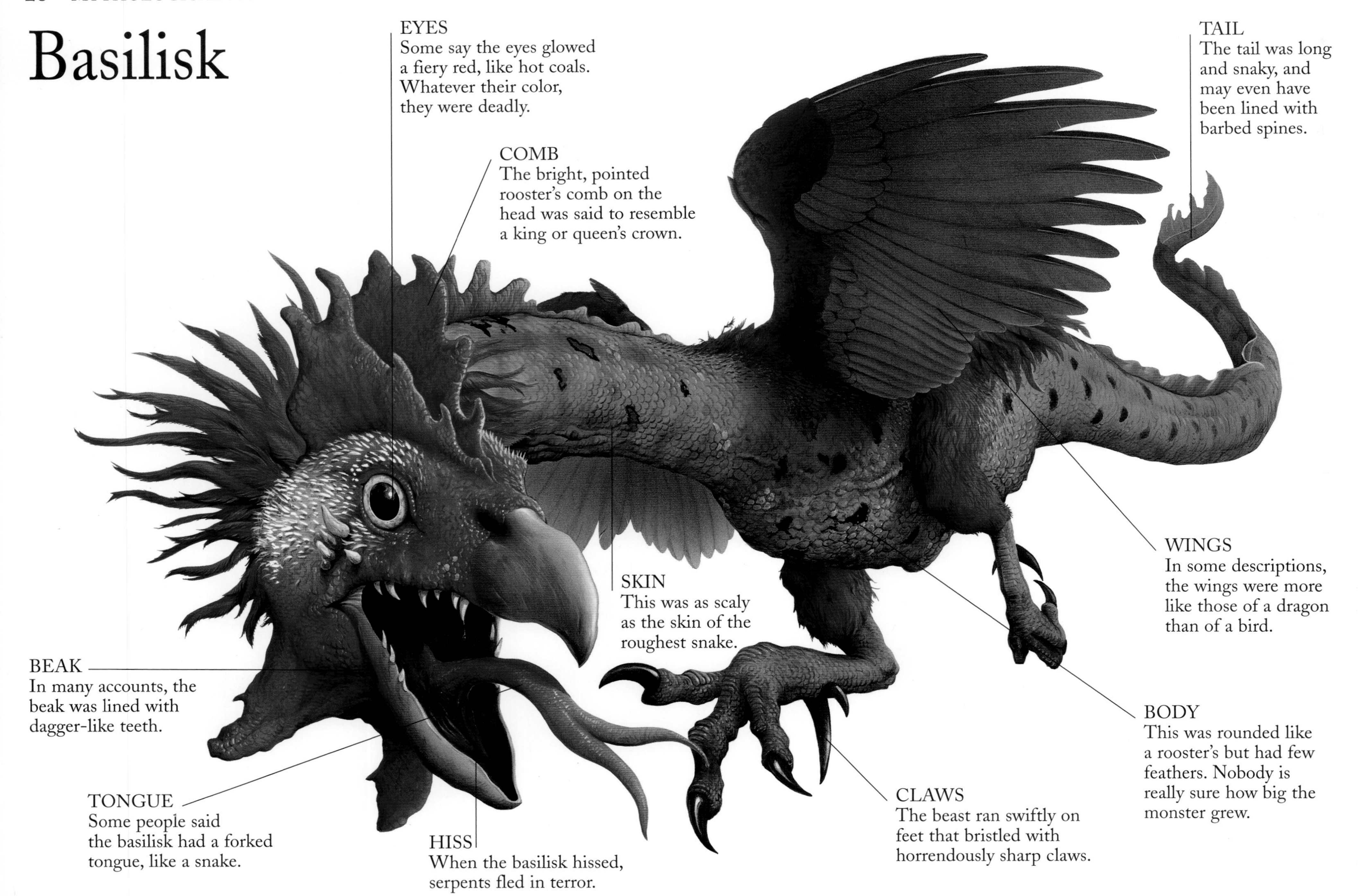
EYES
Some say the eyes glowed a fiery red, like hot coals. Whatever their color, they were deadly.
COMB
The bright, pointed rooster's comb on the head was said to resemble a king or queen's crown.
TAIL
The tail was long and snaky, and may even have been lined with barbed spines.
WINGS
In some descriptions, the wings were more like those of a dragon than of a bird.
SKIN
This was as scaly as the skin of the roughest snake.
BEAK
In many accounts, the beak was lined with dagger-like teeth.
BODY
This was rounded like a rooster's but had few feathers. Nobody is really sure how big the monster grew.
TONGUE
Some people said the basilisk had a forked tongue, like a snake.
HISS
When the basilisk hissed, serpents fled in terror.
CLAWS
The beast ran swiftly on feet that bristled with horrendously sharp claws.

The basilisk was a horrific mix of reptile and bird. It was said to be hatched from an egg laid by a cockerel, an egg that was then incubated by a toad. With their snake-like bodies, cockerel heads and stumpy wings, basilisks had terrifying magical powers. Just the stare of a basilisk could kill people, as could its foul poisonous breath. It polluted waterways and turned green, fertile farmland into nothing but barren desert. Rocks would shatter if the basilisk brushed against them. There were few ways to kill a basilisk. Weasels were said to be immune to basilisk magic and poison, and if a basilisk was confronted with a mirror, it would be killed by its own reflection.

ACTUAL SIZE

▶ A FRESH SOURCE OF TERROR IS ABOUT TO EMERGE INTO THE WORLD. A toad has carefully tended a strange egg abandoned in a grassy field. The warty amphibian watches as first cracks, then a hole appear in the shell. Soon a bird-like head pops out, but this is no fluffy, harmless chick. Moments later, the toad keels over, stone-dead; it is the first victim of a new basilisk's deadly gaze.

Where in the world?

The Roman writer Pliny described the basilisk nearly 2000 years ago, but the creature may be even older. People throughout Europe walked in terror of meeting it right up until the 16th century, when the famous naturalist Konrad Gesner denounced it as "gossip."

Did you know?

- In Warsaw, Poland in 1587, a basilisk was blamed for killing two small girls in a cellar. Reportedly, a "volunteer" prisoner sent down into the cellar killed the creature with a mirror.

- The basilisk myth may come from early reports of hooded cobras, venomous Indian sn rear up and flare a hood of skin. The idea that a weasel can kill a basilisk may com the mongoose, a small mammal that preys on cobras.

Cerberus

MANE
A mane of vipers' heads seethes around Cerberus's neck. In moments of aggression, this mass of snakes bristles and hisses in expectation of violence.

SERPENT TAIL
In the most terrifying portrayals of Cerberus, its tail consists of a serpent whose head rears up and springs into the attack. In other versions, Cerberus has either one or three dragon tails, each bearing a vicious spike.

JAWS
The jaws dribble venomous foam and a foul stench pours from the mouths. The dreadful teeth tear at pitiful victims condemned to punishment.

CLAWS
Some descriptions of Cerberus claim that the clawed feet are used to rip and flay the bodies of people who were [illegible]dy in life.

Cerberus is a particularly ancient mythical "hell hound"—his name is first seen in literature dating from around 700 BC. He is also the ultimate guard dog. In Greek mythology, this three-headed beast presided over the entrance to the Underworld, preventing the unfortunate dead from ever escaping back into the the world of the living. Each terrifying head had powerful jaws that dripped poisonous saliva. A crop of snakes on the top of the heads added to Cerberus' ferocity.

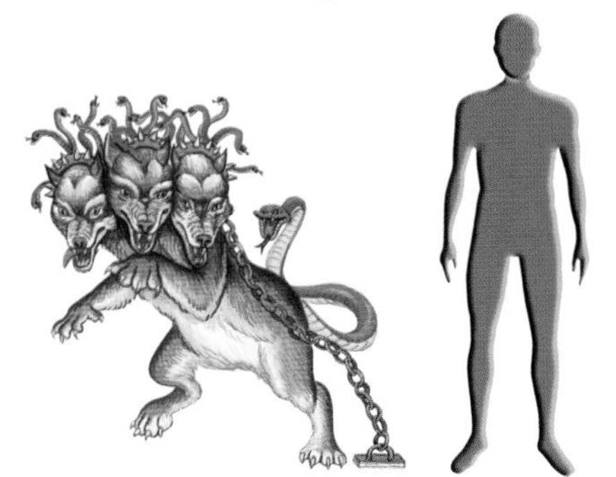

ACTUAL SIZE

▶ The Underworld: In ancient myth, the dead were brought to the bank of the River Styx by the god Hermes. The only way to cross the Styx was to pay the hideous ferryman, Charon. Those who couldn't pay, or who were unburied, were doomed to wander the dismal shore of Styx for eternity. On the far bank, the souls passed Cerberus, who made sure they did not flee back to the land of the living. Once inside the gates of hell the souls were judged for their behavior in life: the good passed to the eternal paradise of the Elysian Fields, while the guilty were doomed to everlasting torment in Tartarus.

Where in the world?

The Ancient Greeks believed that the Underworld lay at the center of the Earth and was accessible through certain entrances. The most famous of these were at Heraclea on the Black Sea and via the River Acheronin Thesprotia.

Did you know?

- Cerberus's name probably stems from the Greek ker berethrou, meaning "demon of the pit."
- The Ancient Greeks were buried with a coin either in the mouth or placed in the grave because they believed their souls had to pay Charon to cross the River Styx.
- When Heracles captured Cerberus, drips of foam from its slavering jaws and venom from its mane of snakes' heads fell on the ground. From these drips sprouted the poisonous plant aconite, commonly known as wolfsbane.
- Theseus, famous for killing the Minotaur, spent four years trapped in hell, continually savaged by Cerberus. He was freed when Heracles captured Cerberus.
- Cerberus's mother was the half-woman, half-serpent, Echidne.

Cyclops

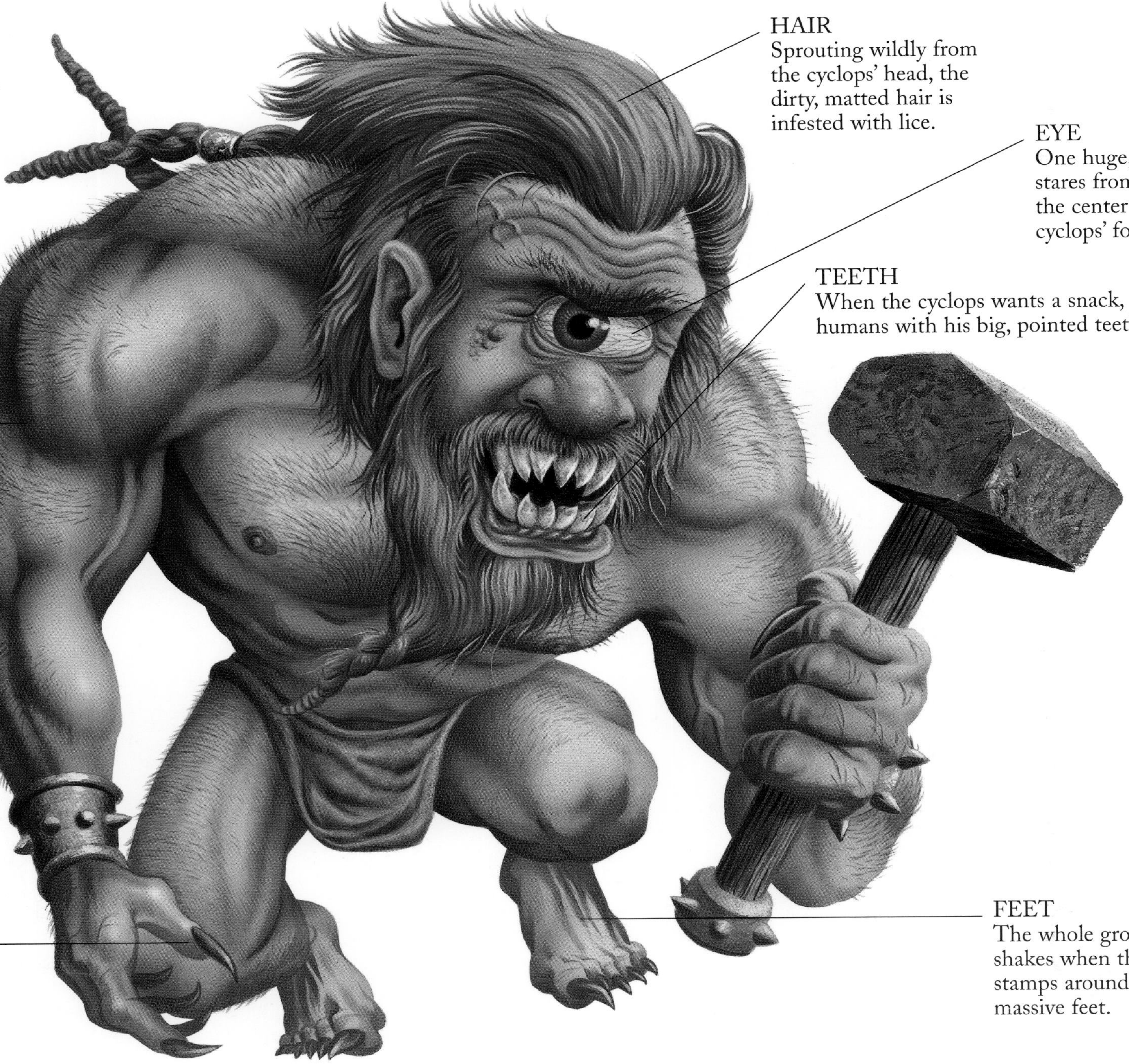

HAIR
Sprouting wildly from the cyclops' head, the dirty, matted hair is infested with lice.

EYE
One huge, watchful eye stares from the center of the cyclops' forehead.

TEETH
When the cyclops wants a snack, he rips up humans with his big, pointed teeth.

ARMS
Bulging with muscles, the long arms pound out metal and shift stone blocks with ease.

CLAWS
Instead of nails, hooked claws grow from the fingers and toes. If the cyclops is in a bad mood, these make formidable weapons.

FEET
The whole ground shakes when the cyclops stamps around on his massive feet.

The single eye of the cyclops stares menacingly from its horrible, hairy face. This cruel, watchful giant can smash a human to pieces with a single flick of the wrist. In Greek mythology, the first cyclopes were three brothers called Steropes, Brontes, and Arges, sons of Ge (Mother Earth) and the god Uranus. They were blacksmiths by trade. The last race of cyclopes were brutish shepherds who lived squalid lives in dingy caves in Sicily, tending their flocks and tearing intruders apart. They communicated with grunts and roars. The cyclops Polyphemus was the most dreadful of all. When Odysseus and his men showed up at his cave, Polyphemus imprisoned them, removing the brains of two men a day.

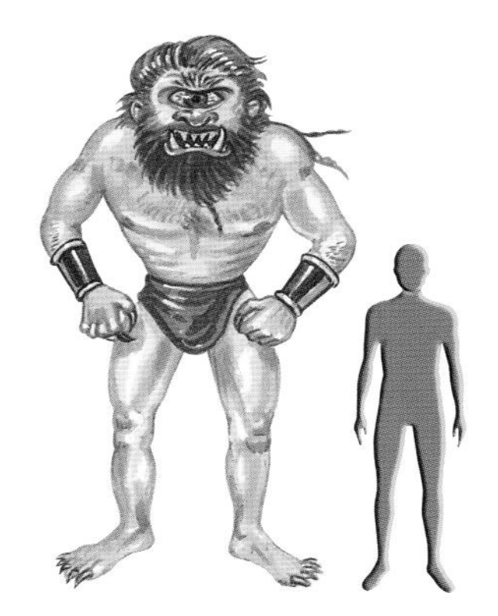

ACTUAL SIZE

▶ ODYSSEUS WAITED PATIENTLY FOR THE CYCLOPS TO FALL ASLEEP. Then the hero sharpened a stake and heated it in the fire. Driving the weapon into the scary giant's eye, Odysseus twisted the stake around, blinding Polyphemus. The survivors escaped the next day, clinging to the bellies of the cyclops' sheep as he sent them out to graze.

Where in the world?

Cyclopes lived in the regions of Thrace in northeast Greece, in Lycia in southwest Turkey, and on the island of Crete. They worked in Hephaestus' forge on Lemnos and built the cities of Mycenae and Tiryns. Later tales place them on Mount Etna in Sicily.

Did you know?

- The word "cyclops"comes from the Greek words kyklos ("circle") and ops ("eye"). The names of the cyclopes Brontes, Steropes, and Arges meant "thunder," "lightning bolt," and "lightning flash."

- The cyclops myth may have its origins in an ancient guild of Greek metal workers in Thrace, who had circles tattooed on their foreheads.

- Some people believe that the legend of the cyclopes arose when the Ancient Greeks first encountered elephants.

Fafnir

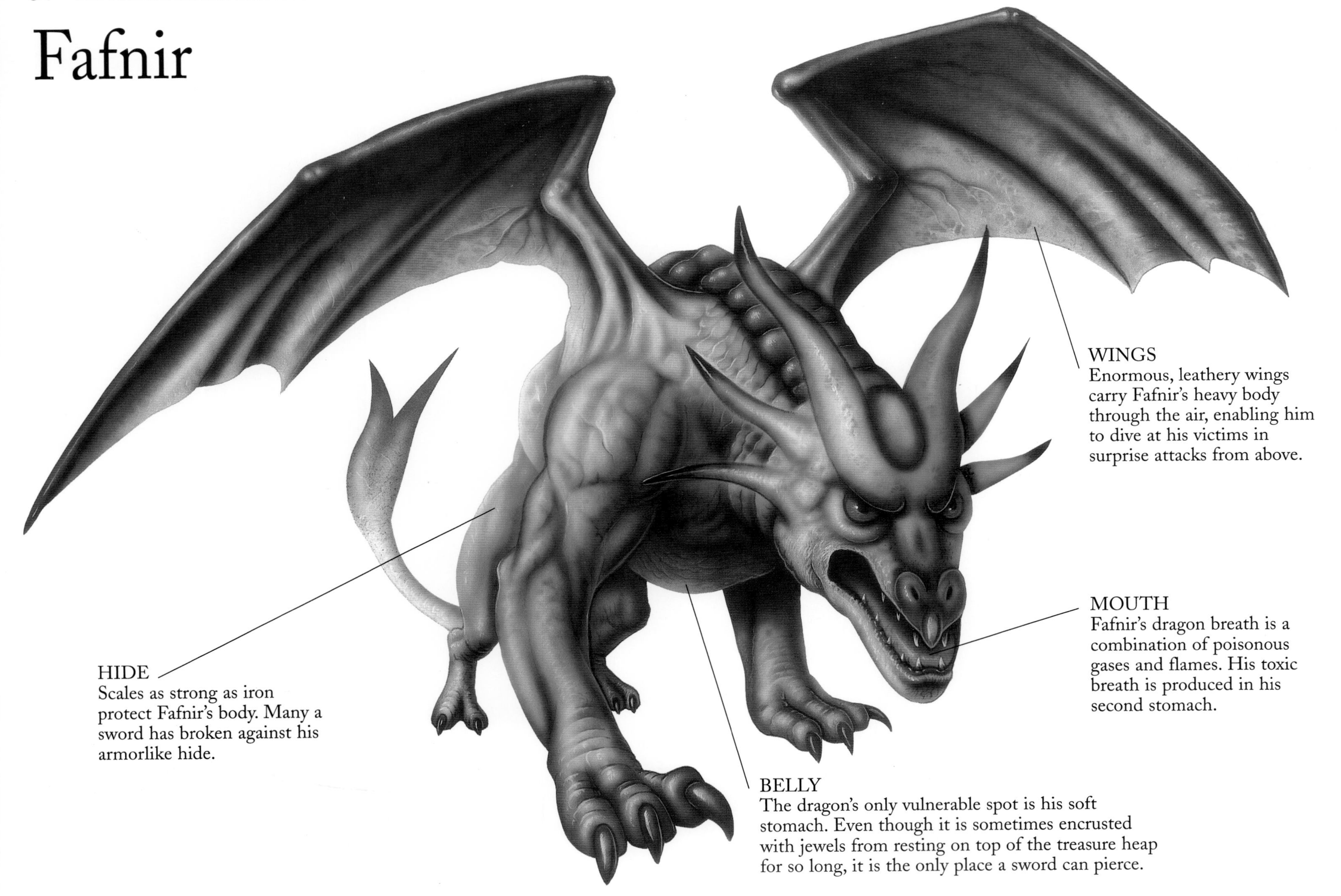

WINGS
Enormous, leathery wings carry Fafnir's heavy body through the air, enabling him to dive at his victims in surprise attacks from above.

MOUTH
Fafnir's dragon breath is a combination of poisonous gases and flames. His toxic breath is produced in his second stomach.

HIDE
Scales as strong as iron protect Fafnir's body. Many a sword has broken against his armorlike hide.

BELLY
The dragon's only vulnerable spot is his soft stomach. Even though it is sometimes encrusted with jewels from resting on top of the treasure heap for so long, it is the only place a sword can pierce.

Fafnir is a simple dwarf warped by greed. Fafnir and his brother Regin want a share of their father's treasure. Fafnir murders his father for the treasure and refuses to share with Regin. Years of gloating over his treasure transform Fafnir from a dwarf into a terrible dragon. Still hungry for a share of the treasure, Regin asks the hero Sigurd to slay Fafnir. The hero needs a reliable sword because the dragon's scales are impenetrable. Numerous swords have already shattered against them. Sigurd repairs his father's broken sword, making it unbreakable and sturdy enough to split an anvil.

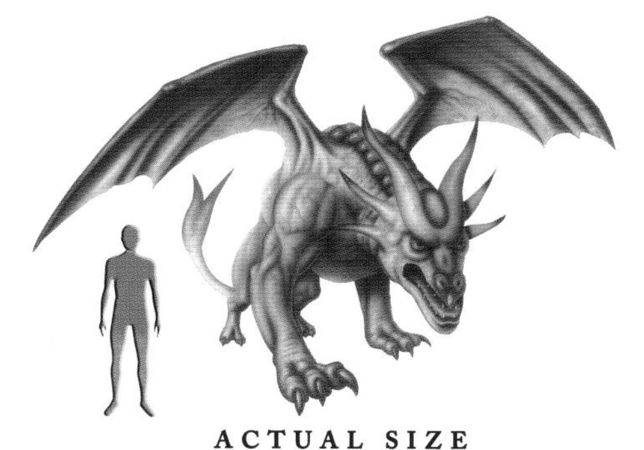

ACTUAL SIZE

▶ SIGURD DIGS A TRENCH ACROSS THE PATH Fafnir follows for his daily drink at the river. Hidden in the trench, Sigurd thrusts his mighty sword into Fafnir's belly as he slithers overhead. At Regin's request, Sigurd cuts out Fafnir's heart and roasts it. Sigurd burns his fingers on the red-hot heart. When he sucks on his fingers to relieve the pain, the taste of Fafnir's blood gives Sigurd the power to understand the language of birds. The birds warn Sigurd that Regin plans to kill him, so Sigurd kills Regin and claims the treasure.

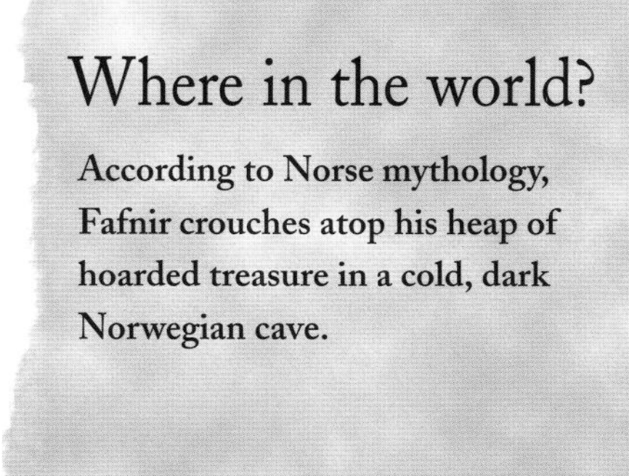

Where in the world?

According to Norse mythology, Fafnir crouches atop his heap of hoarded treasure in a cold, dark Norwegian cave.

Did you know?

- Until Sigurd came along, Fafnir was thought to be undefeatable. Numerous brave men went seeking the dragon's treasure but were burned alive and eaten.

- Fafnir's father was the king of Dwarf Folk. Several Norse gods gave Fafnir's father his treasure as payment for accidentally killing one of Fafnir's brothers.

- The sword that Sigurd has repaired in order to slay Fafnir was once his father's. It was broken when his father battled Odin, the chief god in Norse mythology. As his father lay dying, he predicted that his unborn son would one day forge a powerful weapon from the fragments of his broken sword.

Futs-Lung

BODY
Futs-Lung can transform himself into any shape he desires or make himself completely invisible. He creates new hills when he hunches his back underground.
FIN
The scalloped dorsal fin along the length of his back stabilizes the dragon as he maneuvers through the air, water, and earth at lightning-fast speeds.
EYES
The dragon's bulging eyes can see into the depths of the earth where his treasure is stored.
CHIN
Hidden beneath his chin is the pearl of wisdom. The pearl glows from within and is a vessel of health.
JAWS
Futs-Lung's voice is like the jingling of copper pans, banging gongs, or ringing bells, depending upon his mood. His furious roar brings forth earthquakes.

The dragon of hidden treasures that lives deep within the Earth is Futs-Lung. He guards all the precious gems and priceless metals in his lair. Futs-Lung possesses a magic pearl that multiplies when touched. Since the pearl represents wisdom, it is considered the most valuable of all his treasures. It takes 3,000 years for Futs-Lung to grow to his terrific adult size. Newly hatched, he looks much like an eel. By 500 years of age, Futs-Lung has grown a head that resembles a carp's. By his 1,500th birthday, he will grow a long tail, a head with a thick beard, and four stumpy legs with claws. At the age of 2,000, Futs-Lung will have horns.

ACTUAL SIZE

▶ IN MODERN-DAY HONG KONG there is an apartment complex that was built near a mountain where Futs-Lung lives. The complex was designed with a large gap in the middle so that Futs-Lung's ocean view would remain unobstructed and his goodwill would be maintained. Like most Chinese dragons, Futs-Lung is benevolent until offended. His wrath should not be roused. He must be treated with respect and reverence so he does not unleash his incredible temper. Volcanoes are formed when Futs-Lung bursts from the earth and reports to heaven.

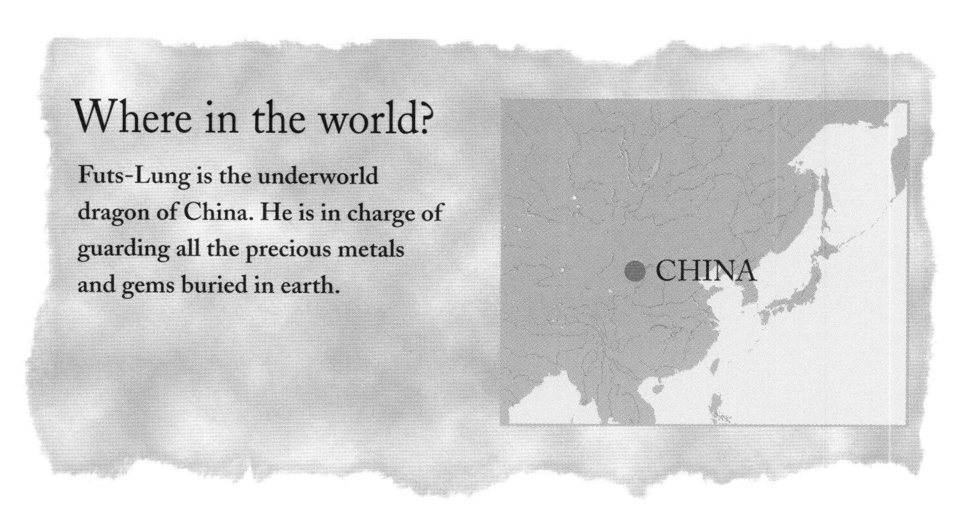

Where in the world?

Futs-Lung is the underworld dragon of China. He is in charge of guarding all the precious metals and gems buried in earth.

Did you know?

- Imperial Chinese dragons have five toes, Korean dragons four, and Japanese dragons three.
- Chinese dragons lay one egg at a time. Each dragon egg takes 1,000 years to hatch.
- The Chinese refer to themselves as "descendants of the dragon."
- Chinese dragons have 117 scales on their serpentine bodies.
- It was a compliment to refer to someone as "dragon face" in China. Many founding emperors of dynasties were described as having dragon faces. It was considered a lucky sign indicating their future greatness.
- Chinese dragons are shape-shifters that can change into the form of a man, shrink themselves down to a mouse, or expand until they fill up the space between heaven and Earth.

Gorgon

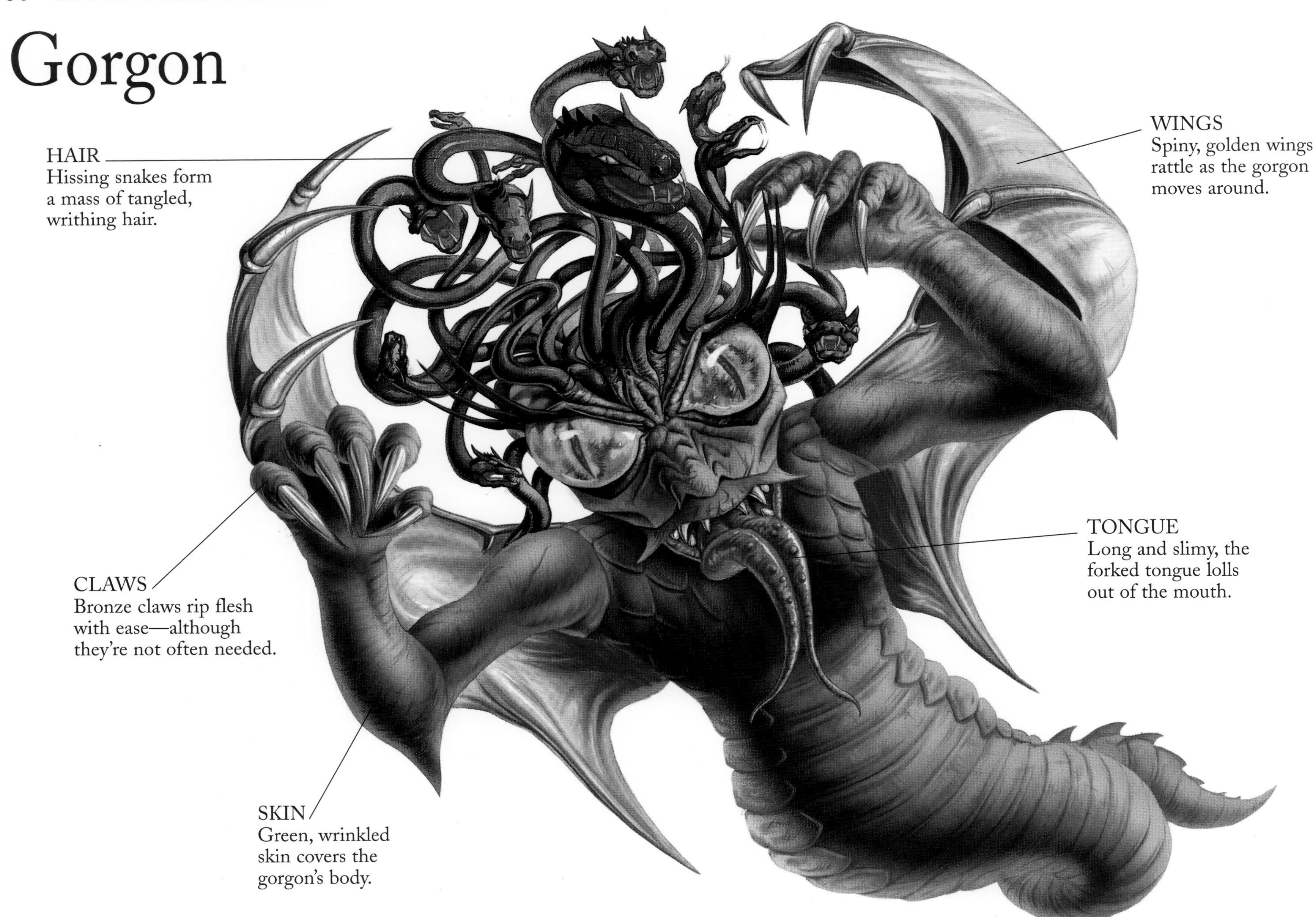
HAIR
Hissing snakes form a mass of tangled, writhing hair.
WINGS
Spiny, golden wings rattle as the gorgon moves around.
CLAWS
Bronze claws rip flesh with ease—although they're not often needed.
TONGUE
Long and slimy, the forked tongue lolls out of the mouth.
SKIN
Green, wrinkled skin covers the gorgon's body.

A gorgon is such a hideous sight that one glance is enough to turn onlookers to stone. The gorgons were not always vile monsters. Once they were beautiful sisters, until Medusa offended the goddess Athena by seducing the sea god, Poseidon, in one of her temples. Athena was furious and turned the sisters into hideous creatures. The hero, Perseus killed the gorgon Medusa with help from the gods and from a highly polished shield. The shield acted like a mirror, which meant he did not have to look directly into Medusa's face. Perseus then used Medusa's severed head to turn his own enemies into statues.

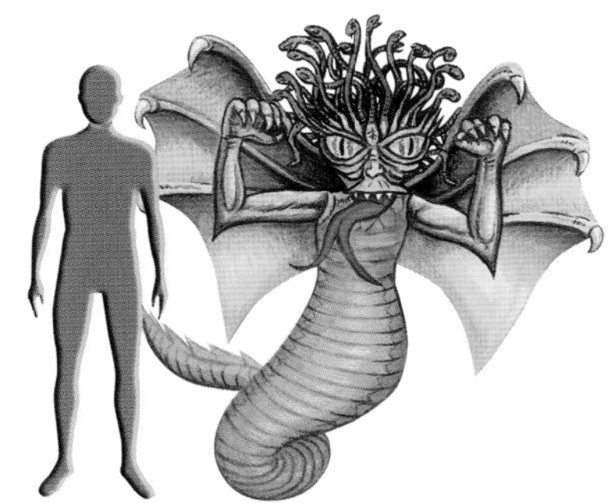

ACTUAL SIZE

▶ MEDUSA IS THE ONLY MORTAL GORGON. Her name means "the cunning one." In some versions of the myth, she is the only one of the three who can turn people to stone, but other versions say that all the gorgon sisters have this power. Stheno and Euryale are Medusa's sisters, destined to share her awful fate. Both of these gorgons are immortal, and in some versions of the myth, are slightly less hideous than their sister. The name Stheno means "the mighty one," and Euryale "the wide-roaming one." Crumbling stone statues litter the gorgons' dreary lair, the petrified remains of onlookers who fell victim to the sisters' terrible powers.

Where in the world?

The ancient Greeks believed the gorgons lived in the mythical land of the Hyperboreans, beyond the north wind on the shores of the ocean that encircled the Earth. The sources place this land as being the coast of Russia, Scandinavia or northeastern Europe.

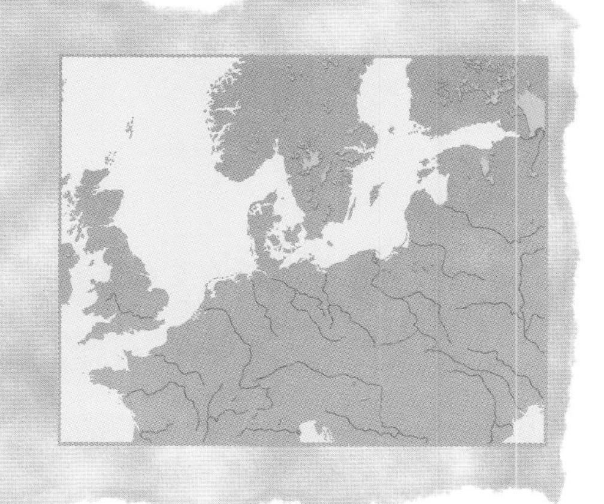

Did you know?

- According to legend, when Perseus cut off Medusa's head, the winged horse Pegasus and a fully armed warrior named Chrysaor sprang from her body.
- As Perseus flew back to Greece, drops of Medusa's blood fell into the sea, instantly turning into coral known as gorgonia. More drops fell on the desert, where they became snakes.
- Athena gave two vials of gorgon blood to Asclepius, the founder of Greek medicine. She filled one from the veins on the left of Medusa's body and the other from the veins on the right. Blood from the left side could raise the dead, while that from the right destroyed life.

Griffin

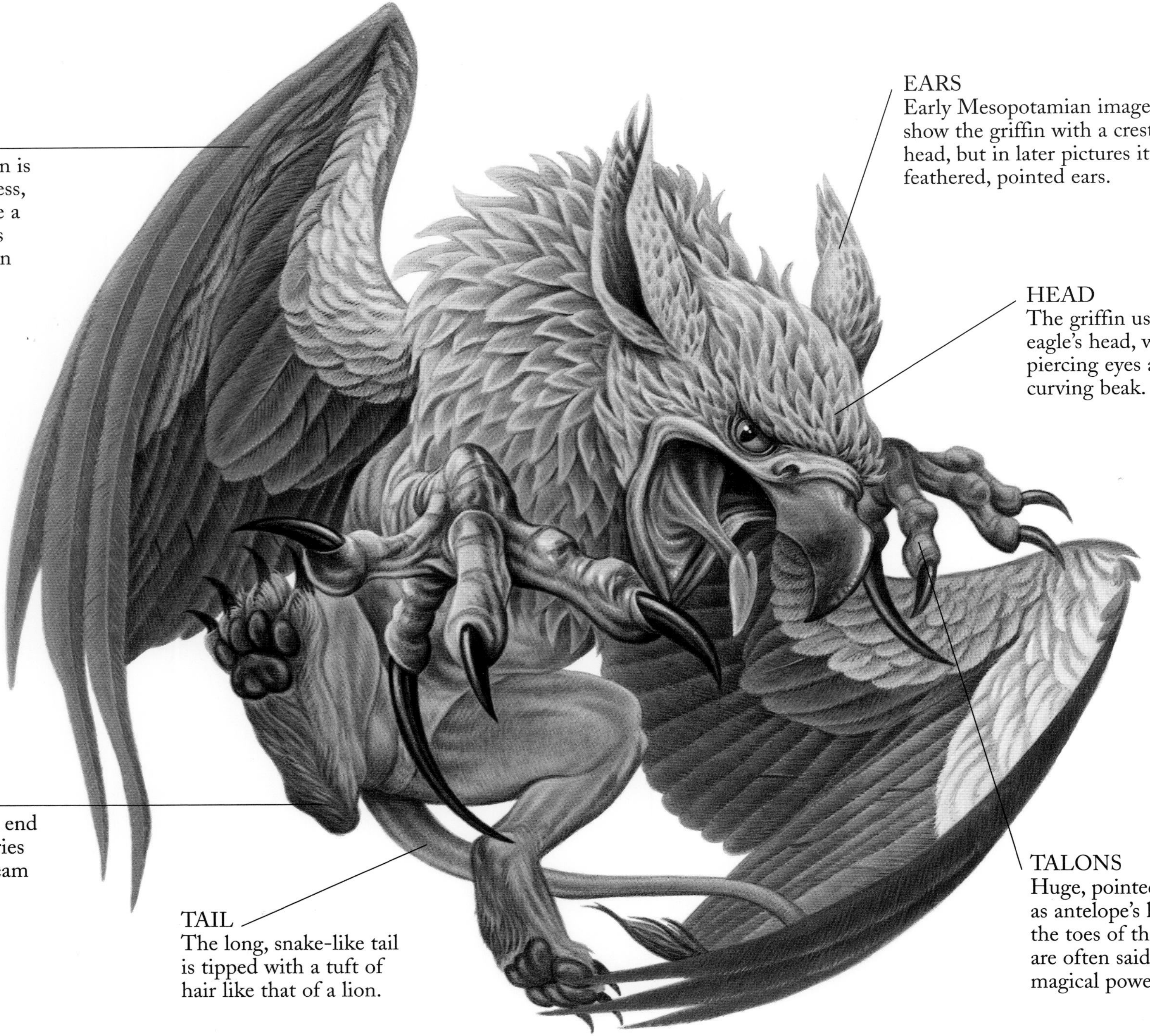

WINGS
Although the male griffin is often described as wingless, the female has wings like a great eagle. In some tales she flies like a bird, but in others she only takes to the air with short hops when fighting.

EARS
Early Mesopotamian images show the griffin with a crested head, but in later pictures it has feathered, pointed ears.

HEAD
The griffin usually has an eagle's head, with terrible piercing eyes and a sharp, curving beak.

HIND PARTS
The griffin has the back end of a lion, and its hair varies in color from gold to cream with scarlet flecks.

TAIL
The long, snake-like tail is tipped with a tuft of hair like that of a lion.

TALONS
Huge, pointed talons as long as antelope's horns grow from the toes of the forefeet. These are often said to possess magical powers.

This ferocious mythological beast has the head, wings and forelegs of an eagle, and the hindquarters of a lion. Given to attacking other animals at will, it's also said to tear up humans on sight with its slashing claws and tearing beak. The griffin is a colossally powerful predator that can carry off a yoke of oxen in its claws—in some medieval accounts, it is stronger than eight lions and 100 eagles. It also hoards gold and emeralds, fiercely attacking anyone who tries to steal from its nest.

ACTUAL SIZE

▶ Many griffins were said to live in the ancient land of Scythia, north of the Black Sea—an area rich in gold and jewels. Digging up these treasures with their claws, they used them to line their nests. The Arimaspians wanted these riches, too, and often rode on horseback into battle with the griffins. As a result, griffins attacked horses whenever they could. Gripping with their scythe-like claws, they hacked in with the hooked bill, leaving terrible, bloody wounds.

Where in the world?

Griffins were thought to live in various parts of the Near and Middle East, from Egypt, Greece, and Turkey to Syria, Iraq, Iran, and Armenia. They were also strongly associated with India and southern parts of the former Soviet Union.

Did you know?

- Artifacts from Ancient Greece sometimes show the griffin with a mane of tightly coiled curls.
- One Norse legend tells of Prince Hagen, who was carried away to a griffin's nest. Fortunately, he found a suit of armor and managed to kill the young griffins as they attacked.
- The female griffin lays eggs, like those of an eagle.

Hatuibwari

HEAD
Four eyes indicate Hatuibwari is wise and all-seeing.
WINGS
Hatuibwari's wings carry him back and forth between the sky and the mountaintops where he lives. Since he has no legs, strong wings are necessary to allow him to hover.
HANDS
The great, clawed hands carefully shaped the first man and woman in Melanesia from clay.
BODY
The serpentine shape of Hatuibwari's torso cuts down on wind resistance and is perfect for darting through the sky. It is also an advantageous design for swimming rapidly through seas.

On San Cristobal Island in Melanesia, the ancient belief is that the dragon, Hatuibwari created and nourished all living things. He is the male version of Mother Earth, with a body that is half-human and half-snake. Two enormous wings carry him through the skies and four eyes allow him to see everything under the Sun. Hatuibwari rolls red clay in his hands, breathes on it, and forms the shape of a human. He places the clay figure in the Sun and it comes to life as the first woman. Later, while the first woman is asleep, Hatuibwari takes a rib from her side, adds more clay, and creates the first man.

ACTUAL SIZE

▶ ONE DAY HATUIBWARI coils around his human grandson to comfort him. The child's father comes home and mistakes Hatuibwari for an enormous serpent squeezing the life from his child. The frightened father does not recognize the dragon spirit as his father-in-law and cuts Hatuibwari to pieces with a knife. The pieces unite again at once. Angry and offended, Hatuibwari announces that he is leaving and will cause the people's crops to fail. Hatuibwari departs to live on Guadalcanal Island and everything deteriorates in his absence.

Where in the world?

The Hatuibwari lives in the sky and on sacred mountaintops of San Cristobal and Guadalcanal in the Solomon Islands, Melanesia.

Did you know?

- The Hatuibwari often appears in a sacred grove. Anyone who does not treat the grove with proper reverence and respect is stricken with illness and terrible sores.

- Sacrifices of pigs are offered to Hatuibwari to appease him. Like Chinese and Japanese dragons, he must be treated with respect or he will grow angry.

- Hatuibwari causes rains to fall in order to quench his thirst.

- Babylonian, Chinese, Australian, and Aztec mythologies all contain stories of dragons as creators of life on Earth.

- In Melanesian mythology, Darkness, Forever, and the Sea have always existed. Hatuibwari created animals, food, trees, and humans. He travels between our world and the sky.

Jawzahr

TAIL
A spade-shaped tuft at the end of his tail indicates Jawzahr is a male. Female dragons lack this tuft.
HEAD
Jawzahr's huge, horned head is able to live independently from his body. His eyes glint with perpetual malice.
JAWS
Gaping jaws capable of devouring the Sun or Moon in one gulp produce a furious screech that can be heard across a continent.
CLAWS
Used for grasping tree branches or stone outcroppings back when he lived on Earth, Jawzahr's claws now grip at the air in a blind rage as he flies through the night skies.
WINGS
Essential to carry him on his unceasing pursuit of the Sun and Moon, Jawzahr's wings contain a structure of lightweight but durable bone. A membrane of leathery skin is stretched across the framework of bone, giving Jawzahr the best aerodynamics of any known dragon.

In ancient Persia, eclipses occur when Jawzahr the comet dragon swallows the Sun or Moon. He menaces the two great luminaries, chasing them around the sky and devouring them at regular intervals. Jawzahr commands a legion of demons and is a crafty, curious dragon. He disguises himself as a god one day and drinks an immortality-giving potion meant only for the gods. The Sun and Moon, however, see everything and they report Jawzahr's trickery to the gods. As punishment, Jawzahr's head is severed with one well aimed throw of a discus. But Jawzahr is already immortal because of the potion he drank and cannot be killed.

ACTUAL SIZE

▶ ENRAGED, JAWZAHR ASCENDS TO THE SKY. The two immortal parts of him live on separate from each other. Jawzahr is angry at both the Sun and Moon for revealing his deception to the gods. He forever chases the Sun and Moon, gobbling them down when he catches them. Any time an eclipse occurs, it means that Jawzahr has caught up with and consumed the Sun or the Moon. As for his tail, it emits a shower of comets that stream across the night sky.

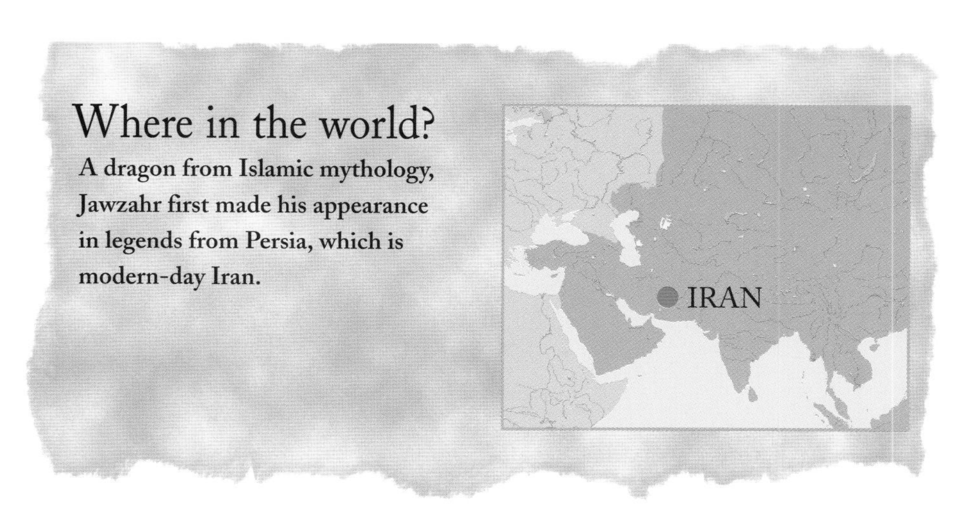

Where in the world?

A dragon from Islamic mythology, Jawzahr first made his appearance in legends from Persia, which is modern-day Iran.

Did you know?

- The astronomical location of the dragon's head and dragon's tail mark the points where solar and lunar eclipses may occur.

- Draco, a constellation in the northern hemisphere, gets its name from the Latin word for dragon. One of the brightest stars in Draco is in its tail and is named Thuban, which is the Arabic word for dragon. Another star in Draco is Rastaban, which means "head of the dragon." About 5,000 years ago Thuban was the Pole Star, Earth's North Star. The ancient Egyptians recognized Thuban as the North Star at the time they were constructing the Great Pyramid. Today our North Star is Polaris.

- Many ancient cultures believed that comets were dragons streaking across the sky.

Kraken

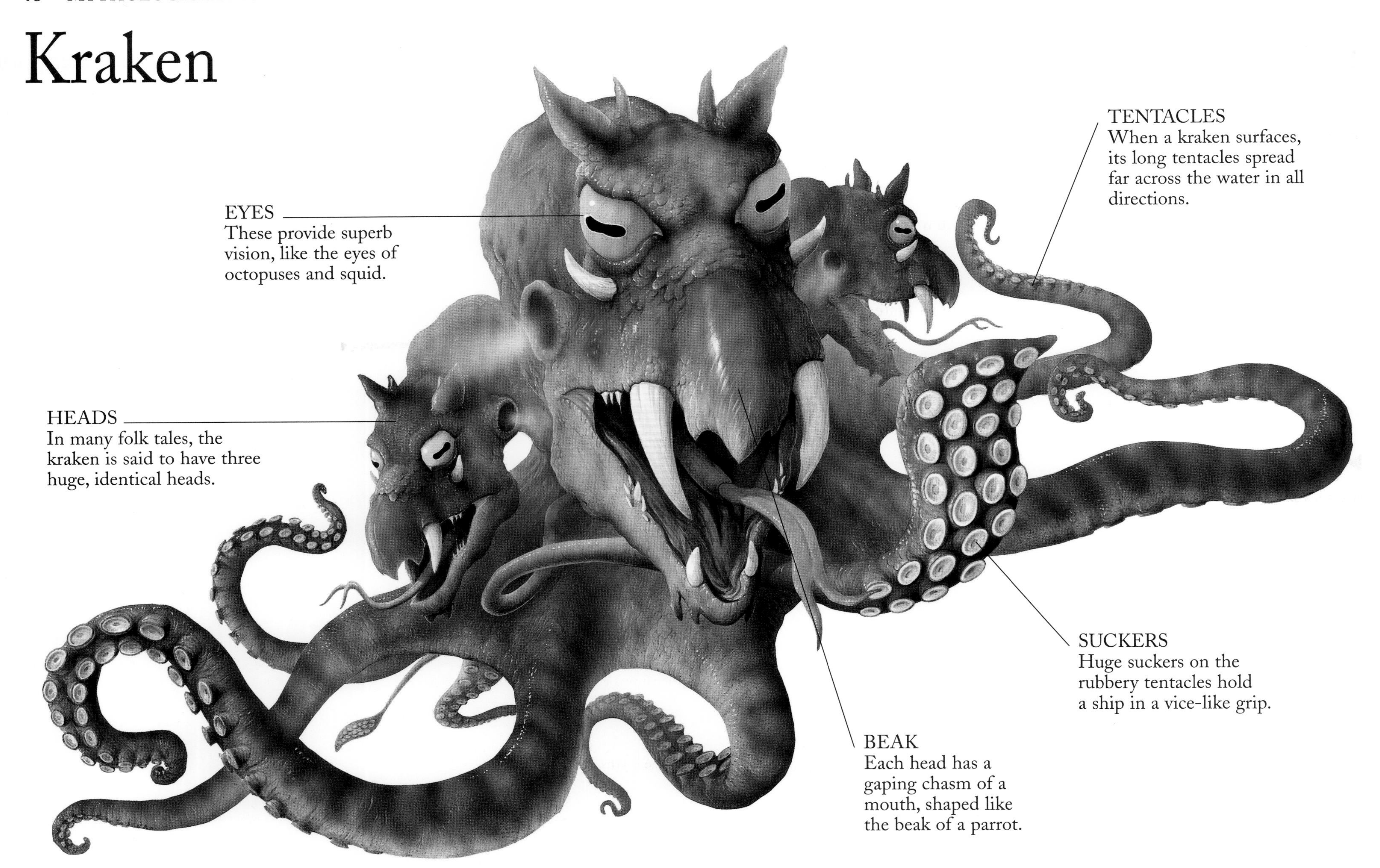
TENTACLES
When a kraken surfaces, its long tentacles spread far across the water in all directions.
EYES
These provide superb vision, like the eyes of octopuses and squid.
HEADS
In many folk tales, the kraken is said to have three huge, identical heads.
SUCKERS
Huge suckers on the rubbery tentacles hold a ship in a vice-like grip.
BEAK
Each head has a gaping chasm of a mouth, shaped like the beak of a parrot.

Since medieval times, sailors and fishermen from western Europe—especially Scandinavia—have told of a vast, tentacled sea monster that lives in the ocean depths. The kraken is a mountain of a creature, dwarfing the largest of whales.

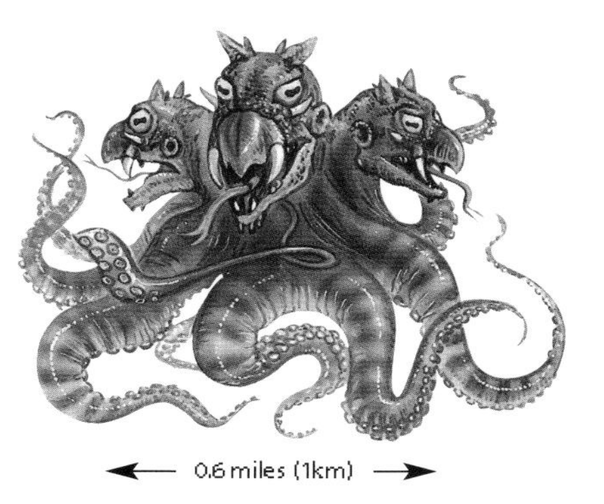

ACTUAL SIZE

In one book on the natural history of Norway, published in 1754, the Bishop of Bergen even claimed that the monster's body was almost 1.5 mi. (2.5km) in circumference.

▶ IN THE SEAS OFF NORTHERN EUROPE, a travel-weary captain sights land at last. His charts make no reference to the strangely rounded islands, but he trusts his eyes and steers his ship toward them. But as he draws closer, the captain realizes his mistake with horror. The "islands" erupt from the sea to reveal a huge kraken. The waking monster seizes the ship in a mighty tentacle and plunges it beneath the boiling waves. Grasping one of the crew with another, it lifts him, screaming, into a gaping beak.

Where in the world?

Most of the legends tell us the kraken lived around the coasts of Scandinavia, especially in the deep waters off Norway. But similar tales also come from other coastal areas of Europe.

Did you know?

- In some tales, the kraken has 1000 tentacles and 10 mouths.
- There are reports of accidental kraken strandings. In 1680, a young kraken supposedly died after it was caught on the reefs off Alstadhang in Norway. And in 1775, another was found on the Isle of Bute in Scotland.
- The English 19th-century poet, Alfred Lord Tennyson wrote a poem, "The Kraken," inspired by the myths.

Ladon

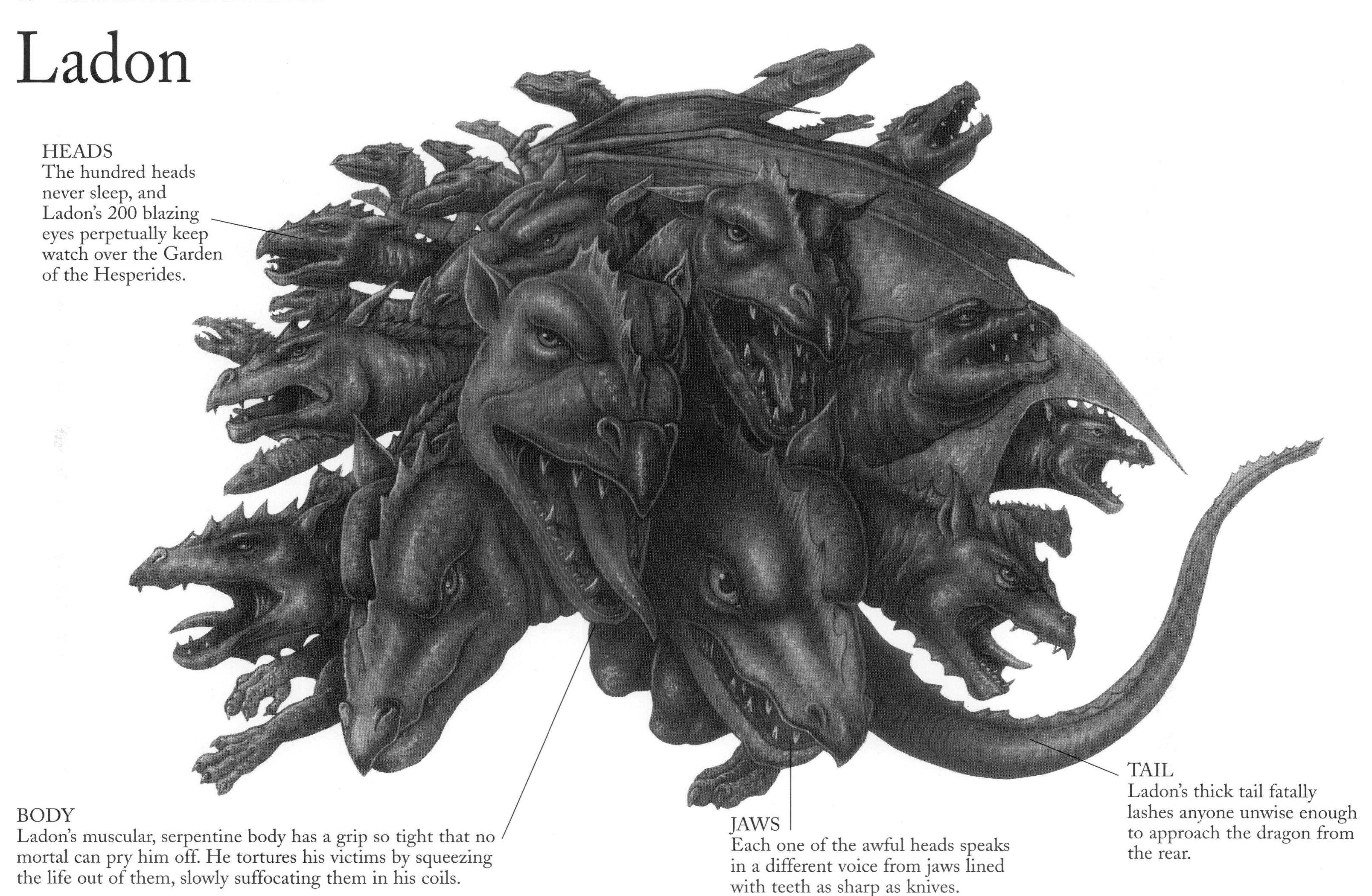
HEADS
The hundred heads never sleep, and Ladon's 200 blazing eyes perpetually keep watch over the Garden of the Hesperides.
BODY
Ladon's muscular, serpentine body has a grip so tight that no mortal can pry him off. He tortures his victims by squeezing the life out of them, slowly suffocating them in his coils.
JAWS
Each one of the awful heads speaks in a different voice from jaws lined with teeth as sharp as knives.
TAIL
Ladon's thick tail fatally lashes anyone unwise enough to approach the dragon from the rear.

In Greek mythology there is a monstrous dragon with 100 heads who twines his serpentine body around a tree bearing golden apples. This beast is Ladon, and he was placed in the Garden of the Hesperides by Hera, queen of the Olympians. His task is to guard the garden and its golden apples. Not one of Ladon's hundred heads ever sleeps and each head speaks with a different voice. Ladon's 200 fiery, watchful eyes ensure that no one approaches the golden apples. Anyone who dares to sail to the ends of the earth in search of Hera's golden apples risks being torn to pieces by Ladon's gigantic teeth or squeezed to death in the coils of his muscular body.

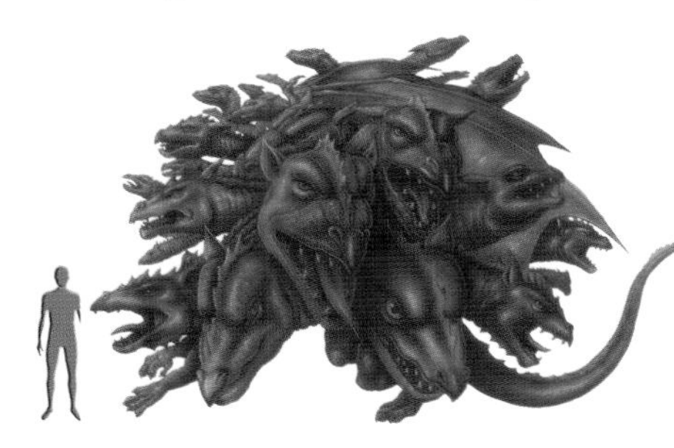

ACTUAL SIZE

▶ THE KING OF MYCENAE TESTS HERACLES by assigning him twelve labors. The eleventh labor requires Heracles to steal the golden apples that Ladon guards. Heracles dips his arrow tips in the gall of a hydra and fires the poisoned arrows over the garden wall at Ladon. The awful dragon is felled by the poisoned arrows and Heracles enters the garden safely. He steals the apples and completes his eleventh labor. Passing sailors later report having seen the slain Ladon with only the tip of his tail still twitching.

Where in the world?

The Garden of the Hesperides, where Ladon winds around the tree of golden apples, lies in the Canary Islands off the coast of Africa, not far from Mount Atlas.

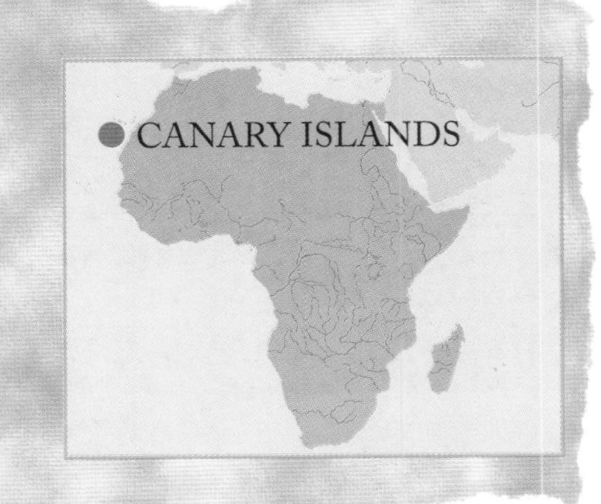

Did you know?

- After his death, Hera places Ladon in the sky as the constellation Draco, where he snakes around the North Pole eternally.
- Where blood from Ladon's wounds drenched the ground, dragon trees sprouted from each drop. Dragon trees have massive trunks and twisted branches. Their sap, called "dragon tree blood," is dark red and is believed to have healing properties.
- In Roman mythology, Heracles is known as Hercules and Hera is called Juno.
- The Latin word for a dragon, "draco," means snake or serpent.
- Direct frontal attack is the least effective way to slay a dragon. Heracles is wise enough to maintain a safe distance from the beast and use the stout garden wall as a shield.

Minotaur

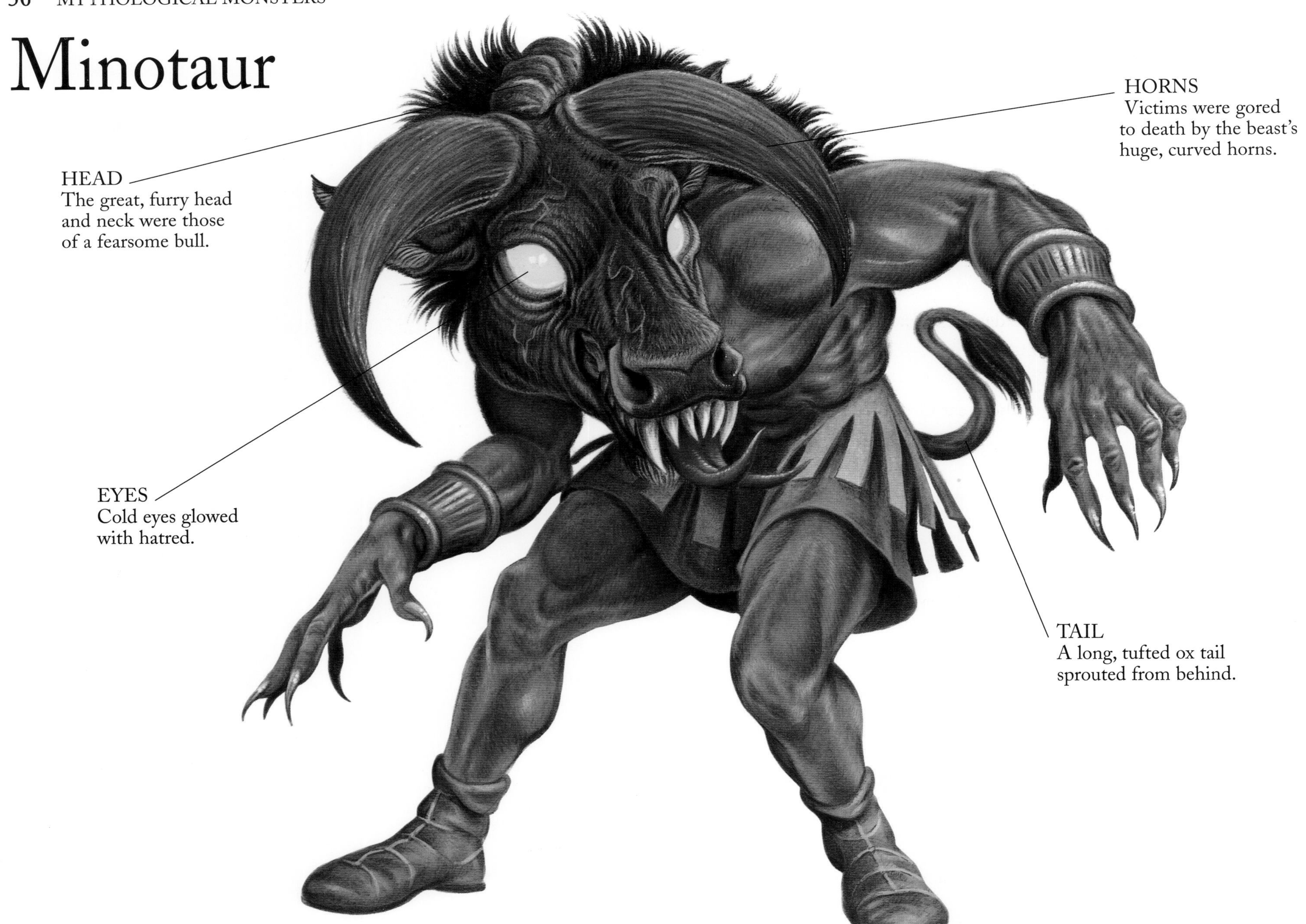
HORNS
Victims were gored to death by the beast's huge, curved horns.
HEAD
The great, furry head and neck were those of a fearsome bull.
EYES
Cold eyes glowed with hatred.
TAIL
A long, tufted ox tail sprouted from behind.

The Minotaur was born after King Minos angered the sea-god Poseidon. Poseidon had sent a snow-white bull for Minos to sacrifice, but Minos couldn't bring himself to kill the bull. Poseidon was furious, and punished Minos by making his wife, Queen Pasiphae, fall in love with the animal. Pasiphae produced a child with a grotesque bull's head and a taste for human flesh. Minos ordered the master craftsman Daedalus to make a vast underground maze to house the monster. The Minotaur was put inside, where it remained lost in the darkness. Every so often, human victims were forced into the maze as sacrifices. The Minotaur was finally vanquished by Theseus, one of the great Greek heroes.

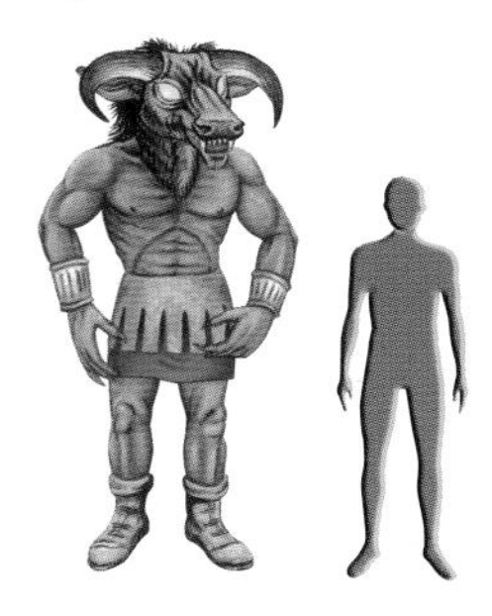
ACTUAL SIZE

▶ THESEUS AND HIS COMPANIONS WERE SENT FROM ATHENS as a sacrifice. Forced into the Labyrinth, they faced a maze of dark passages. Theseus told the Athenians to stay near the entrance while he went in search of the Minotaur, armed with a sword and a ball of thread. Tying the end of the thread to a doorpost, Theseus picked his way through the tunnels of the maze, unraveling the ball as he went. He knew that, after killing the beast, he would be able to retrace his steps and escape the maze by following the thread. Suddenly, the beast was upon him, charging with horns lowered. A fight ensued, until, summoning all his strength, Theseus plunged the sword through the Minotaur's neck, severing its head from its body.

Where in the world?

The mythical Minotaur was said to have lived at Knossos, on the island of Crete in the eastern Mediterranean. Theseus, who slew the beast, came from the city of Athens on the Greek mainland.

Did you know?

- The story of Theseus slaying the Minotaur could be a symbolic version of real historical events, representing the Greek overthrow of Minoan power in 1450 BC.

- Artifacts from ancient Crete show athletes performing the death-defying bull-leaping ceremony. Each athlete would face a wild, charging bull, grasp its spiked horns, and vault or somersault over the animal's back.

- The Nemean lion was another Greek monster: a giant beast invulnerable to wounds.

Oni

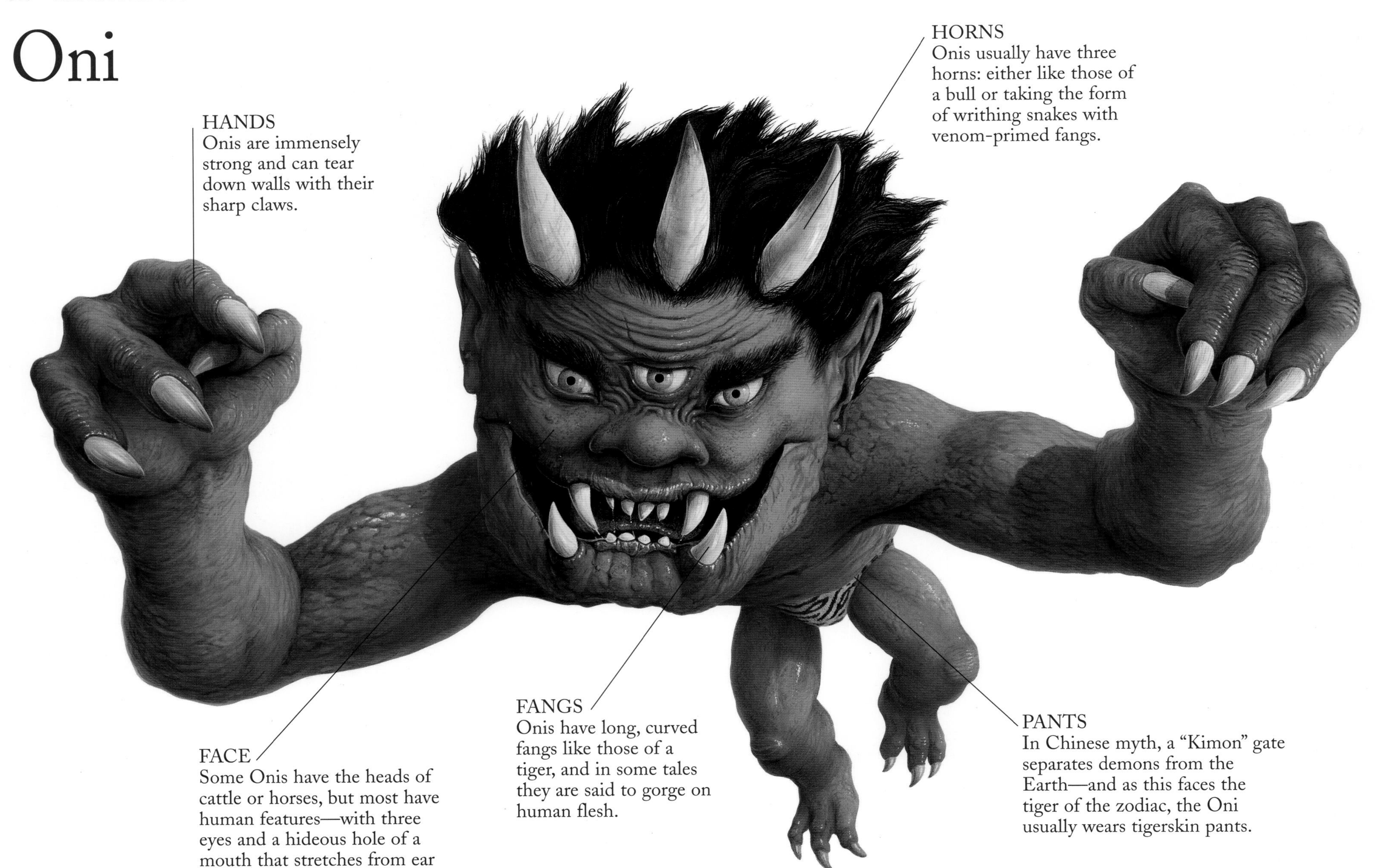

HANDS
Onis are immensely strong and can tear down walls with their sharp claws.

HORNS
Onis usually have three horns: either like those of a bull or taking the form of writhing snakes with venom-primed fangs.

FACE
Some Onis have the heads of cattle or horses, but most have human features—with three eyes and a hideous hole of a mouth that stretches from ear to ear.

FANGS
Onis have long, curved fangs like those of a tiger, and in some tales they are said to gorge on human flesh.

PANTS
In Chinese myth, a "Kimon" gate separates demons from the Earth—and as this faces the tiger of the zodiac, the Oni usually wears tigerskin pants.

Whistling gaily as it works, this ghastly creature delights in tormenting the people of Japan, avoiding detection by flitting invisibly through the air or taking human form. Once a Shinto god, it became an evil spirit after Buddhism spread into Japan from China in the 6th century AD. In earthly guise, it causes disasters, famine and disease, while its demonic form steals sinners' souls. Many Onis have green or red skin. They suffer continual hunger and often have enormous bellies. Hunting down sinners, they take them in a fiery chariot to hell.

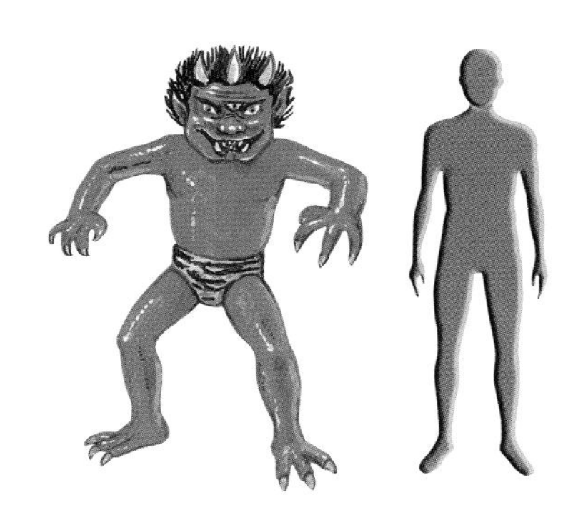

ACTUAL SIZE

▶ THE INHABITANTS OF THIS SMALL JAPANESE VILLAGE are blissfully unaware that the extremely dangerous Oni is hovering above, waiting to cast its evil spell on them. As it swirls above the village considering what damage it can cause, the residents are getting on with their everyday lives, unaware that their lives are about to be completely transformed. What devastation the Oni will bring, nobody knows. Its sheer strength and power could cast a spell causing a terrifying earthquake, a deadly disease or even a terrible famine.

Where in the world?

Onis living in the mortal world are found almost exclusively in Japan, although they are thought to have originated in China. Other Onis known as Gaki inhabit the spirit world or Jigoku (hell) underground.

Did you know?

- A woman may turn into an oni under the stress of jealousy or grief, while other Onis may be the souls of people who died of plague or famine.
- The Buddhist sage Nichiren regarded the Onis as a punishment for the sins of the Japanese, so he founded a school to reform people.
- Although female Onis take the form of beautiful women, they are prone to violent outbursts of rage.

Ryujin

TAIL
A single thrash of Ryujin's tail creates massive tidal waves that wipe out entire coastal villages.

HEAD
His noble head bears the horns of a stag, whiskers that indicate his wisdom, and eyes that see everything from the very bottom of the ocean.

BODY
Ryujin winds his massive, scaly body through the chambers of his underwater palace far beyond the reach of any fisherman or scientist seeking him.

CLAWS
Floods result when Ryujin rakes his impressive claws through the ocean. A swipe of his foot is capable of capsizing an entire fleet of ships.

JAWS
When Ryujin opens his enormous, toothy jaws and inhales, giant whirlpools appear in the water.

In Japanese mythology, Ryujin is the dragon god of the sea. He lives beneath the ocean in a jeweled palace made of red and white coral. His palace has a snowy winter hall, a spring hall where cherry trees grow, a summer hall with chirping crickets, and a fall hall with colorful maple trees. For a human, one day at Ryujin's underwater palace is equal to a hundred years on Earth. Sea turtles, fish, and jellyfish act as the dragon god's loyal servants. Ryujin controls the tides with magical sea jewels. Humans must approach Ryujin carefully because no mortal can glimpse his entire body and survive the sight. When angry, Ryujin churns the waves, causing rough waters for sailors.

ACTUAL SIZE

▶ THE EMPRESS JINGO asks Ryujin for assistance in the attack she plans against Korea. Ryujin's messenger brings her the two tide jewels. Jingo sails toward Korea with the Japanese fleet. The Korean fleet meets them at sea. Jingo flings the low-tide jewel into the sea and all the waters disappear, stranding the Korean ships. When the Korean soldiers leap from their ships to attack on foot, Jingo casts the high-tide jewel onto the seabed. All the waters rush back, drowning the Korean soldiers.

Where in the world?

Ryujin, the dragon god of the sea, lives at the bottom of the ocean near the Ryukyu Islands off the coast of Japan.

Did you know?

- Ryujin's beautiful daughter married Prince Hoori. This makes Ryujin the ancestor of all the Japanese emperors.

- Because Japanese dragons are related to royalty, no one is allowed to harm them. Since they have nothing to fear from humans, Japanese dragons have become tame over the years. Dragons may be seen blocking traffic in cities or sunning themselves on rocks off Japan's shores.

- Many dragons are shape-shifters. They can change into the form of a human, mate, and produce human offspring.

- In both Japan and China, the dragon is one of the guardian animals of the four directions. The dragon guards the eastern compass point and is associated with the season of spring.

Shen-Lung

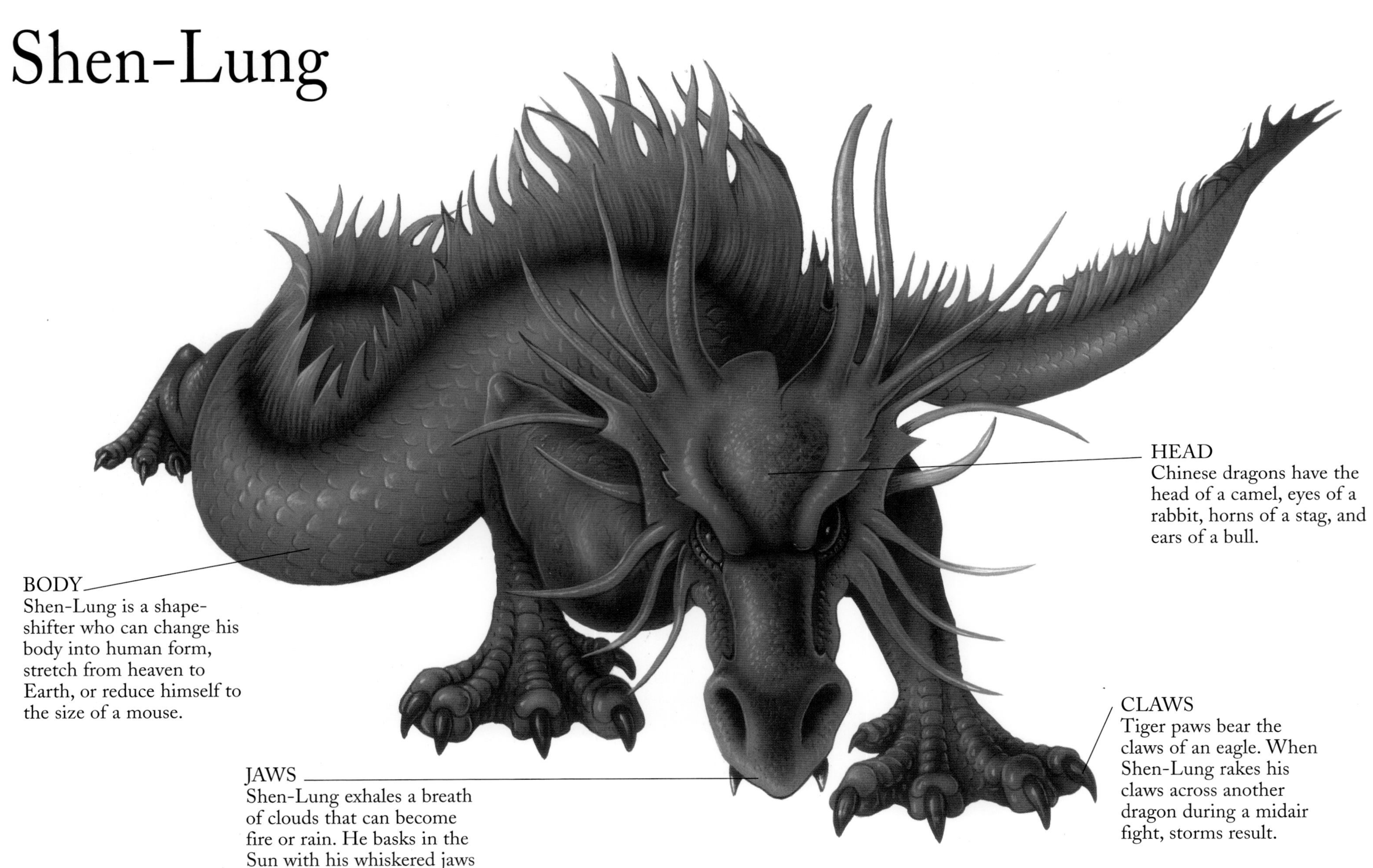
HEAD
Chinese dragons have the head of a camel, eyes of a rabbit, horns of a stag, and ears of a bull.
BODY
Shen-Lung is a shape-shifter who can change his body into human form, stretch from heaven to Earth, or reduce himself to the size of a mouse.
JAWS
Shen-Lung exhales a breath of clouds that can become fire or rain. He basks in the Sun with his whiskered jaws hanging open, hoping that a delicious sparrow will land in his mouth.
CLAWS
Tiger paws bear the claws of an eagle. When Shen-Lung rakes his claws across another dragon during a midair fight, storms result.

In China, Shen-Lung is the spiritual dragon who is responsible for making weather. He controls rain, clouds, and wind, all of which are important in a country with so many farmers. The right amount of rain is essential for healthy crops, so his power over rain gives Shen-Lung the authority over life and death in China. Offerings to Shen-Lung assure a bountiful harvest. He must be approached with the utmost respect and reverence. It is important not to offend Shen-Lung because if he feels neglected his anger is aroused. The result of his wrath is terrible weather in the form of floods or drought, which could destroy the life-giving crops upon which the Chinese depend.

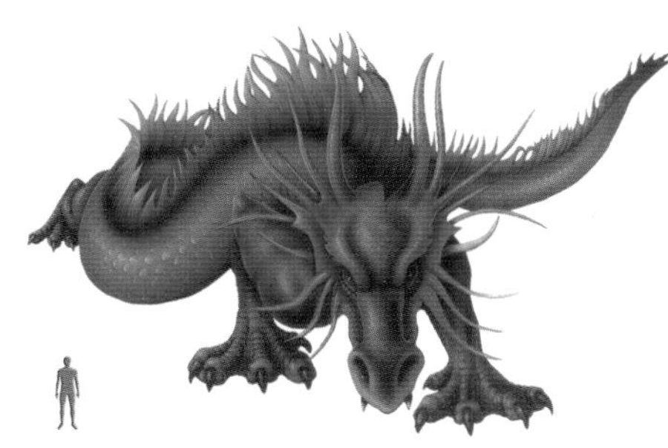
ACTUAL SIZE

▶ BECAUSE OF HIS GREAT POWER, Shen-Lung grows lazy over the years. He shrinks himself to the size of a mouse in order to hide and avoid work. When lightning strikes a house or tree, it is the thunder god sending his servant to search for Shen-Lung. Shen-Lung floats across the sky, his body stretching farther than the eye can see. He is benevolent but bad-tempered. The worst floods in Chinese history were unleashed by Shen-Lung when he was offended by a mortal.

Where in the world?

Shen-Lung is the spiritual dragon who has control over the winds and the rains that affect all the crops grown in China.

Did you know?

- Shen-Lung's voice is heard in hurricanes and his claws can be seen in flashes of lightning.
- When Shen-Lung is sick, the rain has a distinctly fishy smell.
- The dragon is the emblem representing the Chinese emperor and the phoenix represents the empress. Together, the dragon and the phoenix are used as symbols of marital harmony.
- All Chinese dragons have nine distinct features: the head of a camel, scales of a carp, horns of a stag, eyes of a rabbit, ears of a bull, neck of a snake, belly of a clam, paws of a tiger, and the claws of an eagle.
- The dragon ranks first in the Chinese mythological hierarchy of 360 scaled creatures.
- Glass was thought to be solidified dragon breath.

Sphinx

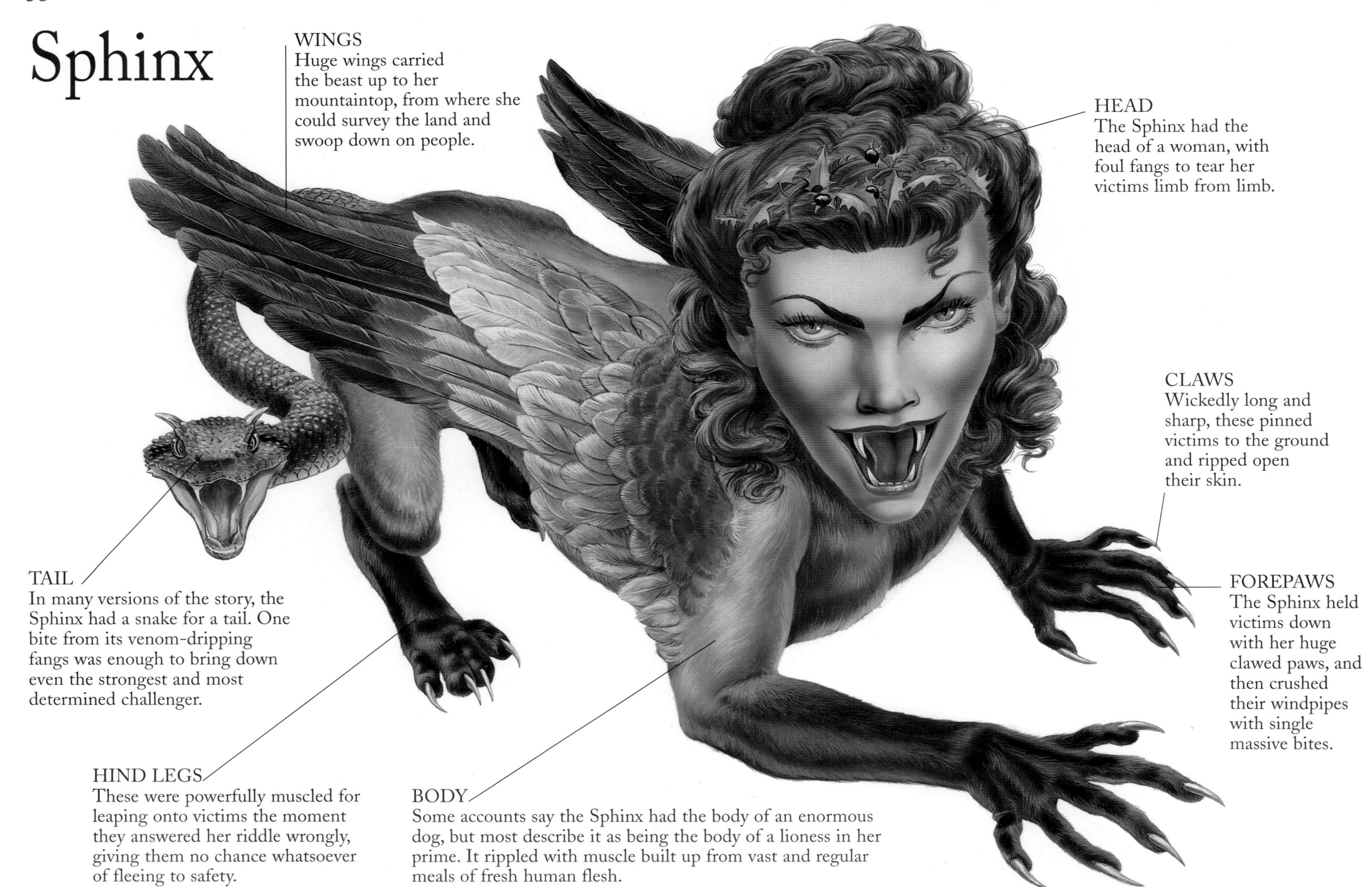
WINGS
Huge wings carried the beast up to her mountaintop, from where she could survey the land and swoop down on people.
HEAD
The Sphinx had the head of a woman, with foul fangs to tear her victims limb from limb.
CLAWS
Wickedly long and sharp, these pinned victims to the ground and ripped open their skin.
FOREPAWS
The Sphinx held victims down with her huge clawed paws, and then crushed their windpipes with single massive bites.
TAIL
In many versions of the story, the Sphinx had a snake for a tail. One bite from its venom-dripping fangs was enough to bring down even the strongest and most determined challenger.
HIND LEGS
These were powerfully muscled for leaping onto victims the moment they answered her riddle wrongly, giving them no chance whatsoever of fleeing to safety.
BODY
Some accounts say the Sphinx had the body of an enormous dog, but most describe it as being the body of a lioness in her prime. It rippled with muscle built up from vast and regular meals of fresh human flesh.

This cruel monster of Greek legend challenged all who tried to pass her to solve a riddle—then slaughtered and devoured them when they got the answer wrong. The Sphinx was a horrible creature with the head of a woman, an eagle's wings, the body of a lioness and a snake for a tail, and she terrorized the poor people of Thebes in Greece from her domain on a mountaintop. She was finally killed by the Greek hero Oedipus, who marched straight up to the monster in her lair on Mount Phicium and demanded to hear her riddle. To her complete amazement, Oedipus answered confidently and correctly: "A man." Enraged, the Sphinx hurled herself off the mountain and fell screaming to her death in the valley below.

ACTUAL SIZE

▶ NO ONE CAN pass the Sphinx unless they correctly answer her riddle. An intrepid traveler approaches. Nervously, he calls out: "Tell me your riddle, O mighty Sphinx." Fixing him with her steely gaze, she chants in a sing-song voice: "What walks with four legs in the morning, two at noon and three in the evening, and the more legs it has the weaker it be?" Trembling with fear, the man suggests "A grasshopper?" "WRONG!" screams the Sphinx and, before the man can escape, she pins him to the ground and clamps her teeth around his throat.

Where in the world?

Depictions of Sphinxes are known from all over the eastern Mediterranean. In the Greek legend, the Sphinx came from Ethiopia and lived on Mount Phicium, which may be Mount Parnassus, in Thebes in Greece.

Did you know?

- "Sphinx" means "strangler" and comes from the ancient Greek verb "sphingo," meaning "to throttle."

- Since it was carved more than 4000 years ago, the Great Sphinx in Egypt has spent most of its time buried up to its neck in sand. The head has been badly worn by weathering and at some point lost its beard and nose. Also, troops of Emperor Napoléon Bonaparte (1769–1821) of France used it for target practice.

Thunderbird

This gigantic two-headed bird-of-prey is known by Native American tribes to bring thunder and lightning to the skies. Lightning bolts shoot from its eyes, storm clouds are carried on its wings, and an entire lake of water on its back makes torrential downpours. Yet in Native American mythology, the thunderbird means different things to different tribes. Some tribes believe that the thunderbird is even the Great Creator Spirit that made the heavens and the earth. Native tribes in Africa and Australia also have similar traditions to the thunderbird, no doubt inspired by the sight of eagles or vultures circling high up in the skies.

ACTUAL SIZE

▶ THE NOOTKA PEOPLE OF VANCOUVER ISLAND, off British Columbia, called the thunderbird Tootooch. To them, it was the sole survivor of four giant birds that preyed on whales. By turning into a whale, the god Quawteaht tricked the birds into attacking him. He lured three to their death as he dived deep, but the survivor flew to the heavens. In the tales of the Quillayute people of the Olympic Peninsula in Washington State, the thunderbird and killer whale are deadly enemies. They once fought a fierce battle, shaking the mountains and uprooting trees, creating vast treeless plains.

Where in the world?

Thunderbirds are part of the belief systems that were held by many different groups of Native Americans, from the Inuit peoples in the Arctic, to the Aztecs in Mexico. These gigantic birds are thought to live either in the sky or in remote mountain caves.

Did you know?

- Many Native American tribes claim to have seen the thunderbird, and in South Dakota they believe it has left huge footprints. The prints are 25 mi. (40 km) apart in an area known as Thunder Tracks, near the source of St. Peter's River.

- Some stories say that the thunderbird lives in a mountain cave, burying its food in a dark hole in the ice. If hunters come too close, it rolls huge lumps of ice down the mountainside to scare them away.

Dracula

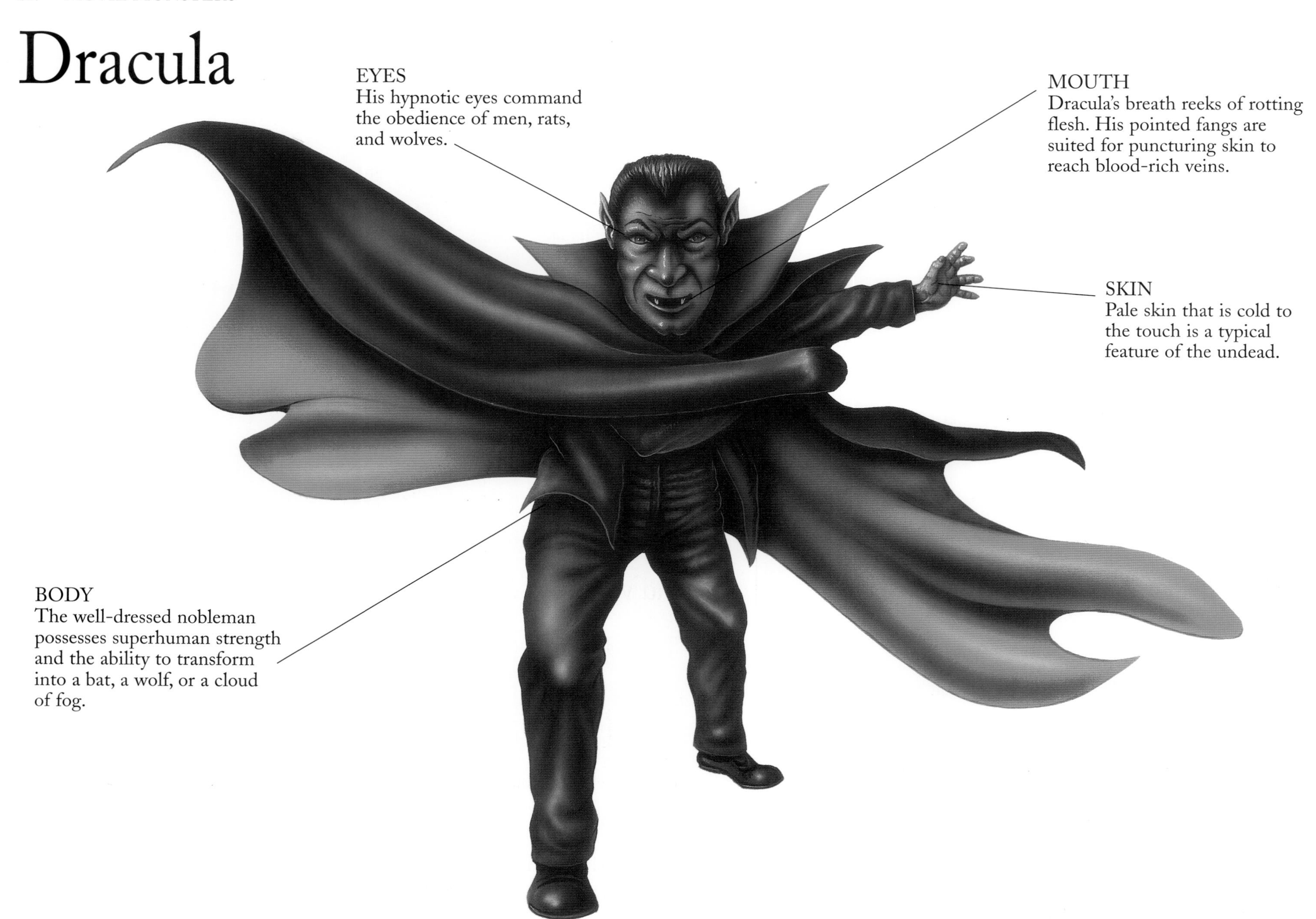
EYES
His hypnotic eyes command the obedience of men, rats, and wolves.
MOUTH
Dracula's breath reeks of rotting flesh. His pointed fangs are suited for puncturing skin to reach blood-rich veins.
SKIN
Pale skin that is cold to the touch is a typical feature of the undead.
BODY
The well-dressed nobleman possesses superhuman strength and the ability to transform into a bat, a wolf, or a cloud of fog.

Count Dracula, the most famous vampire in history, must drink human blood in order to survive. If he does not drink blood regularly, he will begin to age rapidly. Although hundreds of years old, Dracula maintains the appearance of a wealthy middle-aged nobleman thanks to his diet of blood. Elisabeta is the love of his life, and when she dies, Dracula rejects God and curses the living. The count uses black magic to rise from the grave as a vampire. The only companions in his grim, remote castle are his three undead vampire brides. Dracula decides it is time for him to expand his territory and he hires a real estate agent.

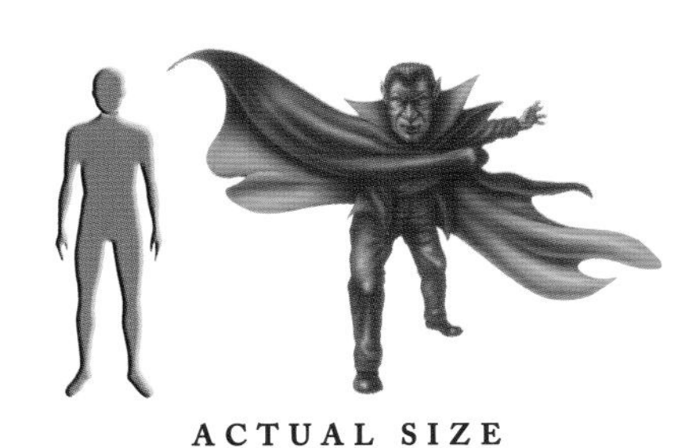

ACTUAL SIZE

▶ DRACULA SETS SAIL FOR LONDON, taking with him coffins containing his native soil. The vampire discovers that Mina, the fiancée of his real estate agent, resembles his long-dead love Elisabeta. Dracula appears in Mina's bedroom at night. He plans to transform her into a vampire with his bite and by feeding her his own blood. Once she is a vampire, Mina will be doomed to drink blood or die. Before she can be fully transformed, Dracula is hunted down. His throat is slashed and he is stabbed through the heart with a knife.

Where in the world?

Dracula's secluded castle is located in the Carpathian Mountains of Transylvania, which is part of modern-day Romania.

Did you know?

- When Dracula is killed, the bite marks on Mina's neck disappear and she is free of the vampire's curse.

- The preferred method of killing a vampire is to drive a wooden stake through its heart and decapitate it to prevent it from returning to life.

- A creature of the night, Dracula is less powerful during the hours of daylight. His otherworldly nature means that the vampire does not cast a shadow and mirrors do not show his reflection.

- Bram Stoker, the author of *Dracula,* was a sickly child. He was bedridden for the first seven years of his life. His mother told him horror stories to entertain him. When he was finally well enough to leave the house, his playground was the local graveyard.

Frankenstein's Monster

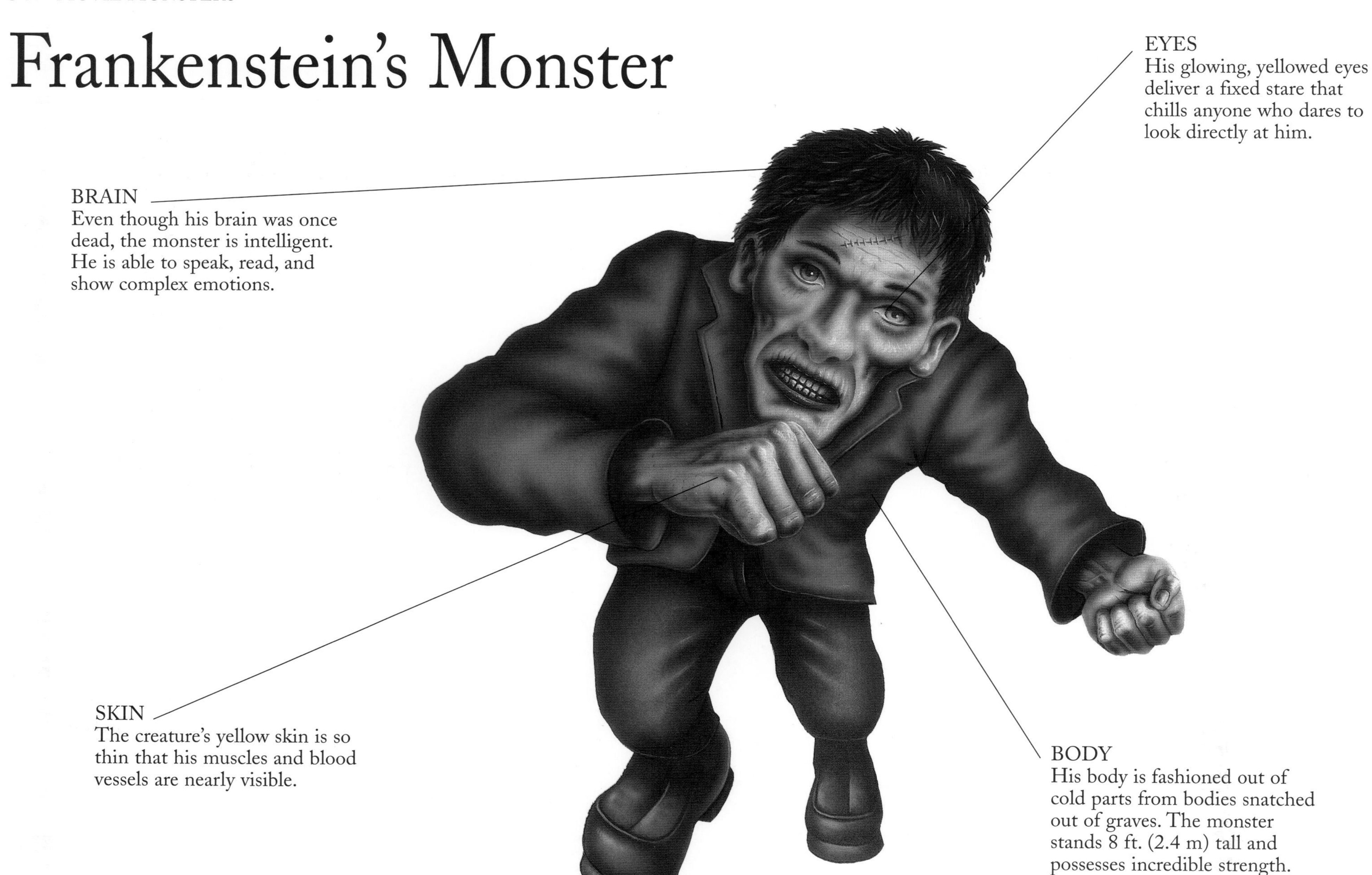

Pieced together from body parts stolen from graves, Frankenstein's monster is a terrible reminder that humans should not attempt to play God. Victor Frankenstein believes that electricity can be used as a power source to bring the dead back to life. He harnesses powers meant only for God, and the result is that he creates a monster which destroys him. Frankenstein conducts a series of experiments on stolen corpses. When a bolt of lightning brings his monster to life in the lab, Frankenstein is immediately sorry. He intended his creation to be beautiful, but it is revolting. Horrified, Frankenstein runs away from his awful creation.

ACTUAL SIZE

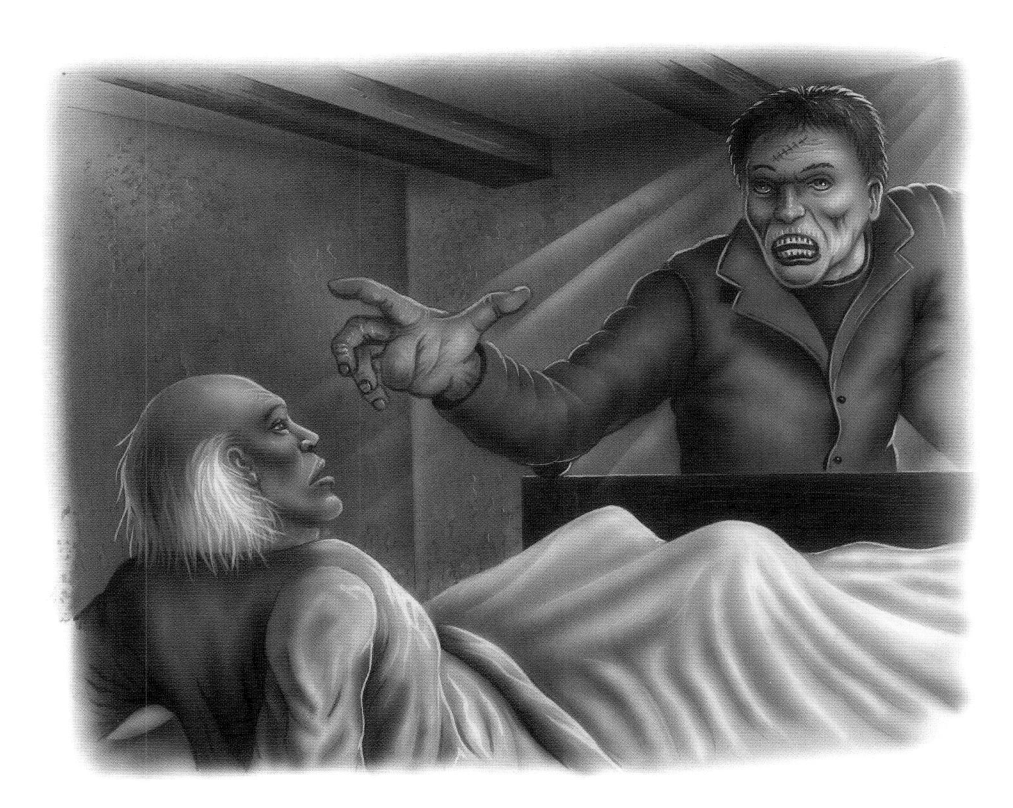

▶ FRANKENSTEIN AWAKES TO SEE THE GHASTLY MONSTER standing at his bedside. Once again, he flees his creation. When Frankenstein's brother is murdered, the monster admits killing him as a way to strike back at his creator for rejecting him. The lonely monster begs Frankenstein to create a mate for him. Frankenstein begins work on a female creature, but his conscience forces him to destroy her and dump her lifeless body in a lake. As revenge, the furious monster murders Frankenstein's bride on their wedding night.

Where in the world?

The secret lab where Victor Frankenstein brings his monster to life is in an unknown location near Geneva, Switzerland.

Did you know?

- Frankenstein spends the rest of his life pursuing the monster to take revenge for the death of his bride. He tracks the creature to the icy Arctic and chases him on a dogsled, but the ice between them separates in a huge crack. When Frankenstein dies, the monster weeps over the body of his creator. The creature heads off across the ice to die alone.

- Mary Shelley wrote the novel *Frankenstein* when she was 19 years old.

- The name "Frankenstein" is often incorrectly used to refer to Victor Frankenstein's creation. Throughout the book, his creation is referred to as "the creature" or "the monster." Frankenstein is the name of the scientist who created the monster.

Glaurung

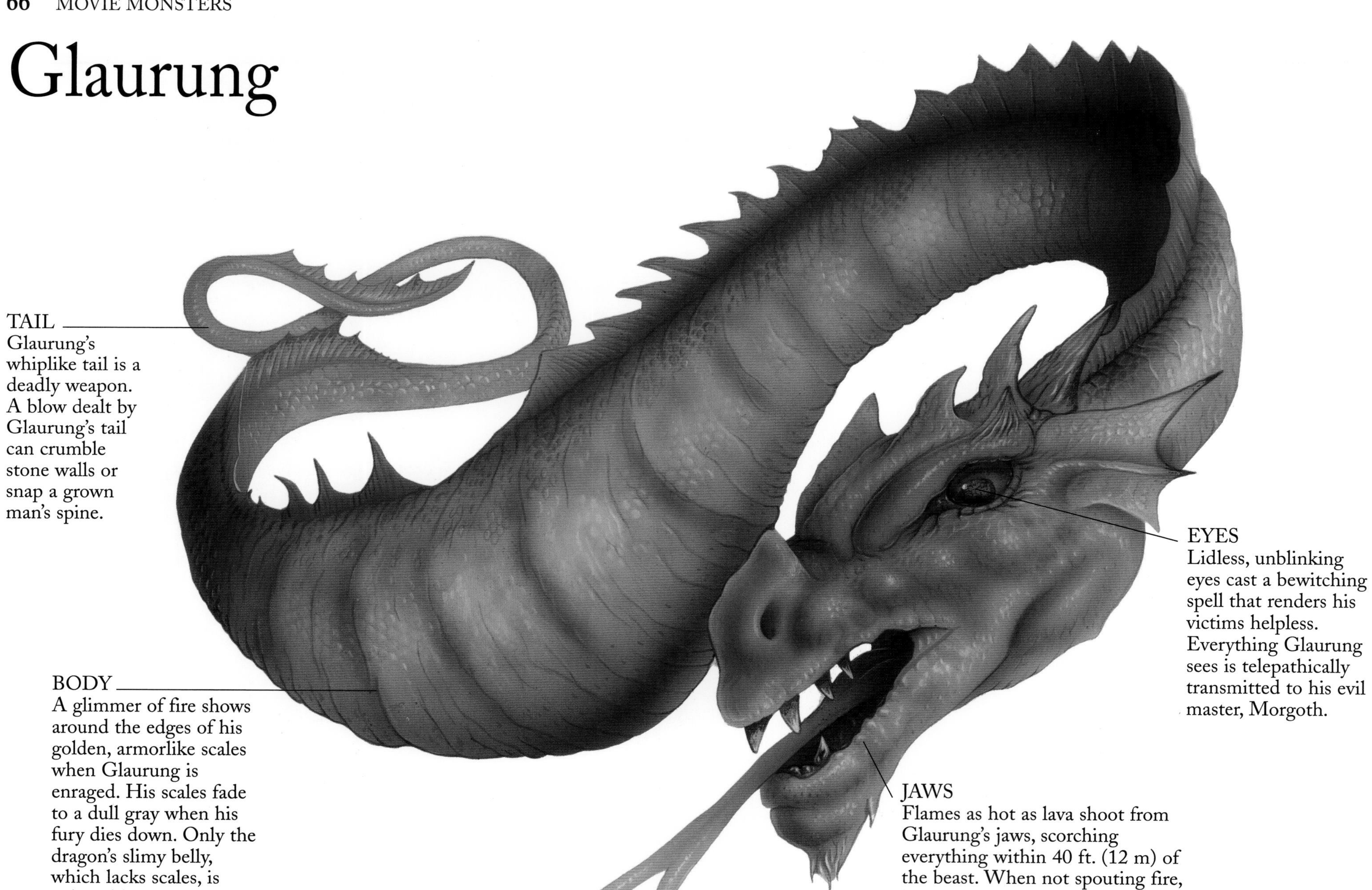

TAIL
Glaurung's whiplike tail is a deadly weapon. A blow dealt by Glaurung's tail can crumble stone walls or snap a grown man's spine.

BODY
A glimmer of fire shows around the edges of his golden, armorlike scales when Glaurung is enraged. His scales fade to a dull gray when his fury dies down. Only the dragon's slimy belly, which lacks scales, is vulnerable to attack.

EYES
Lidless, unblinking eyes cast a bewitching spell that renders his victims helpless. Everything Glaurung sees is telepathically transmitted to his evil master, Morgoth.

JAWS
Flames as hot as lava shoot from Glaurung's jaws, scorching everything within 40 ft. (12 m) of the beast. When not spouting fire, his breath has the distinctly putrid reek of decaying animal flesh.

Glaurung the Deceiver, or the Worm of Greed, is the Father of Dragons. Bred by Morgoth the Enemy, Glaurung uses trickery and deception to spread lies. He enjoys creating misery and confusion in others. The dragon wreaks as much havoc using the spells he casts as he does on the battlefield using brute force. Glaurung is corrupt and foul-smelling, able to taint pure waters with his mere presence. He serves as the eyes of evil Morgoth, who senses everything the dragon sees. Before he is fully mature, Glaurung participates in battle, but his armor is not fully hardened and cannot withstand the archers' arrows.

ACTUAL SIZE

▶ GLAURUNG CASTS DRAGON SPELLS with his lidless, unblinking eyes. He fills the head of the heroic Túrin with lies and self-doubt. Túrin's sister, Nienor, is also victim of Glaurung's spell. She is spellbound with complete forgetfulness and cannot remember her own name. As a result, Nienor unwittingly marries her brother. In order to slay the deceiver, Túrin clings to a cliffside above a deep gorge where Glaurung passes. When the dragon slithers overhead, Túrin kills Glaurung by thrusting his black sword into the beast's soft belly.

Where in the world?

Glaurung is the first and fiercest of the land-dwelling fire drakes of J.R.R. Tolkien's Middle Earth in *The Silmarillion*. Glaurung builds a nest upon the treasure in the tunnels beneath Nargothrond after the city is sacked.

Did you know?

- When Glaurung dies, both Túrin and Nienor are released from the dragon's spell. Both commit suicide when they discover they have married a sibling.

- Blood issues from the fatal wound when Túrin pulls the black sword from Glaurung's body. The poisonous blood burns Túrin's hand.

- Glaurung, red-hot with wrath, lies in a river where he generates a horrible reek and foul vapors that blind people until they lose their way. Even horses are driven mad by the dragon's stench.

- Anyone foolish enough to look Glaurung directly in the eye is immediately rendered helpless by his dragon spell.

- Glaurung led the assault in the Battle of Sudden Flame but was knifed in the belly and had to flee the battlefield to heal.

Godzilla

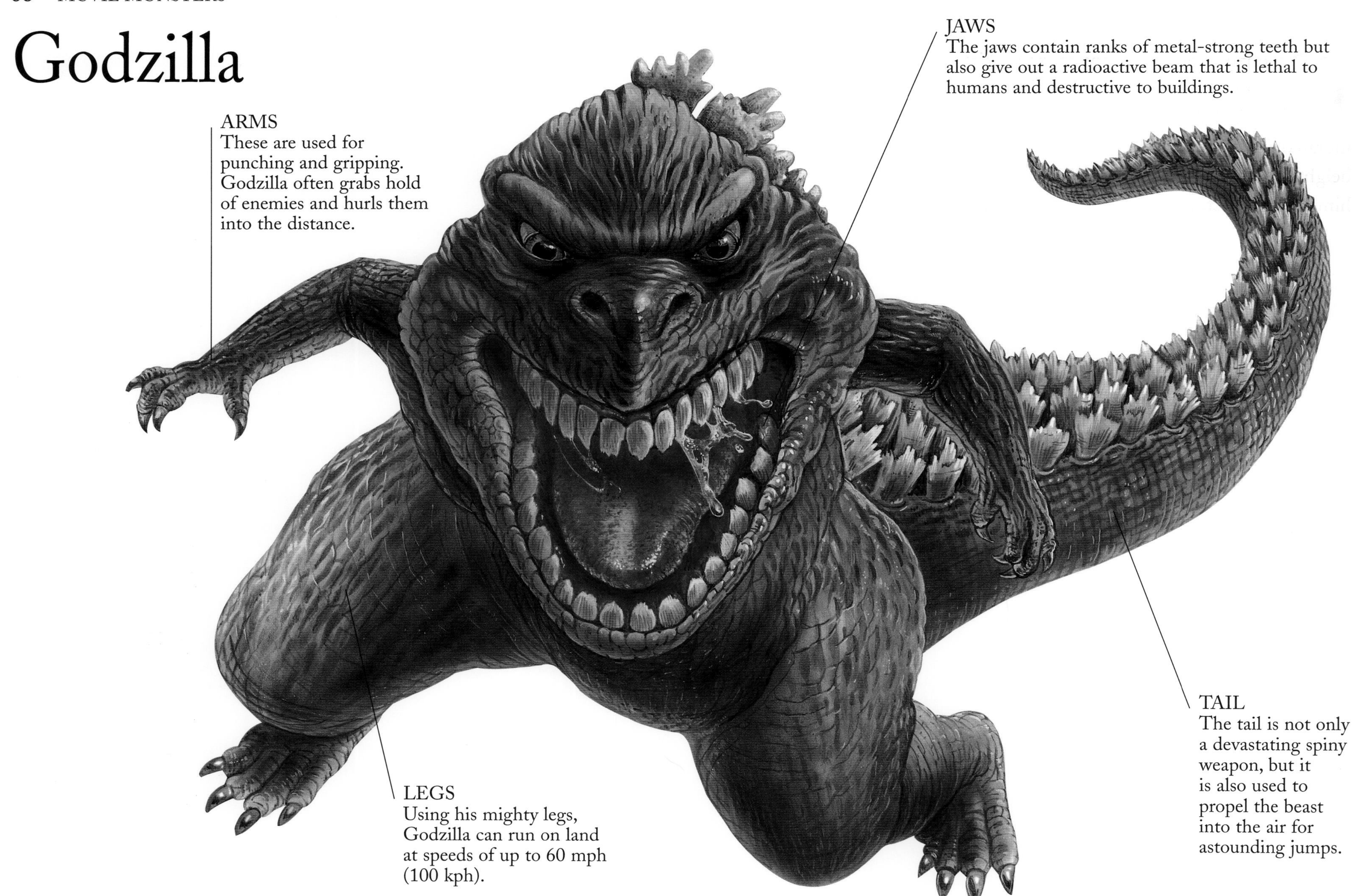

ARMS
These are used for punching and gripping. Godzilla often grabs hold of enemies and hurls them into the distance.

JAWS
The jaws contain ranks of metal-strong teeth but also give out a radioactive beam that is lethal to humans and destructive to buildings.

LEGS
Using his mighty legs, Godzilla can run on land at speeds of up to 60 mph (100 kph).

TAIL
The tail is not only a devastating spiny weapon, but it is also used to propel the beast into the air for astounding jumps.

Godzilla was a remnant of the prehistoric age, a species of dinosaur known as the Godzillosaurus. Injured and awakened by US shelling during the Pacific War, the great beast mutated following later atomic bomb tests in the region and grew to a height of over 300 ft. (91 m). Then, turning upon the world that awoke him from prehistoric slumber, Godzilla unleashes a truly awesome destructive power. He is almost indestructible, with modern bullets and bombs bouncing off his armor-like hide. He also has weapons of his own, including (depending on the storyline) a lethal atomic energy beam that he fires from his vast and gaping jaws.

ACTUAL SIZE

▶ While swimming out at sea—where he moves underwater with the speed of a military submarine—Godzilla spots the sparkling lights of Tokyo on the horizon. He moves toward them, and the Tokyo citizens see his enormous bulk rise out of the harbor waters. Godzilla plunges into the heart of the city, smashing down entire skyscrapers with his tail and crushing cars, trucks and people under his massive feet. Having obliterated much of Tokyo's city center, Godzilla then slips back into the waters and disappears from sight.

Where in the world?

Godzilla has traveled the world in print and film, but his origins lie on the island of Lagos, near the Marshall Islands in the southern Pacific Ocean. It is a tropical region devastated during World War II.

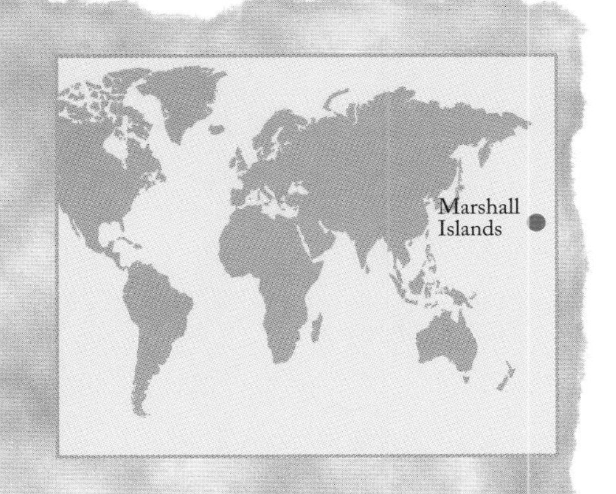

Did you know?

- Godzilla first appeared on movie screens in 1954, the film coming from the Japanese Toho Co. Ltd. His original name was "Gojira," but this changed to Godzilla to meet the needs of American audiences.

- Throughout his monstrous career in film and comic books, Godzilla has battled with numerous monster and alien enemies. His foes include King Kong, Mothra, and Titanosaurus.

- "Gojira" combines the Japanese names for gorilla and whale.

Hungarian Horntail

As the first task of the Triwizard Tournament in J.K. Rowling's *Harry Potter and the Goblet of Fire*, Harry must get past a mother Hungarian Horntail and steal a golden egg from her nest. The golden egg is placed among her clutch of gray eggs. A nesting mother Horntail is especially hazardous when defending her young. Harry summons his racing broom and uses it to fly back and forth, taunting the dragon. He dodges blasts of fire deftly on his broom but has one shoulder scraped by her thrashing, spiked tail. He lures the furious dragon up onto her hind legs by flying high above her, then swoops down and snatches the golden egg.

ACTUAL SIZE

▶ The Hungarian Horntail is remarkably dangerous because it can do as much damage with its spike-lined tail as it can with its fanged mouth, which shoots jets of fire up to a distance of 50 ft. (15 m). The young use their spiked tails to club their way out of their eggs. It can require anywhere from six to eight well-trained wizards to subdue a fully grown Hungarian Horntail with stunning spells. It is considered the most dangerous of all dragon breeds, according to the Ministry of Magic.

Where in the world?

Normally native to Hungary, smuggling of the Hungarian Horntail's eggs has led to sightings of the dragon in England.

Did you know?

- The blood, heart, horn, hide, and liver of dragons all have magical properties.
- There are 10 breeds of purebred dragon that can interbreed and produce hybrid dragons.
- The female dragon is larger and more aggressive than the male dragon.
- The motto for Hogwarts School of Witchcraft and Wizardry—*Draco Dormiens Nunquam Titillandus*—means "Never tickle a sleeping dragon."
- The dinosaur *Dracorex Hogwartsia*, which means "dragon king of Hogwarts," was named by young visitors to the Children's Museum of Indianapolis.
- The Ministry of Magic has classified the Hungarian Horntail as a known wizard-killer.

King Kong

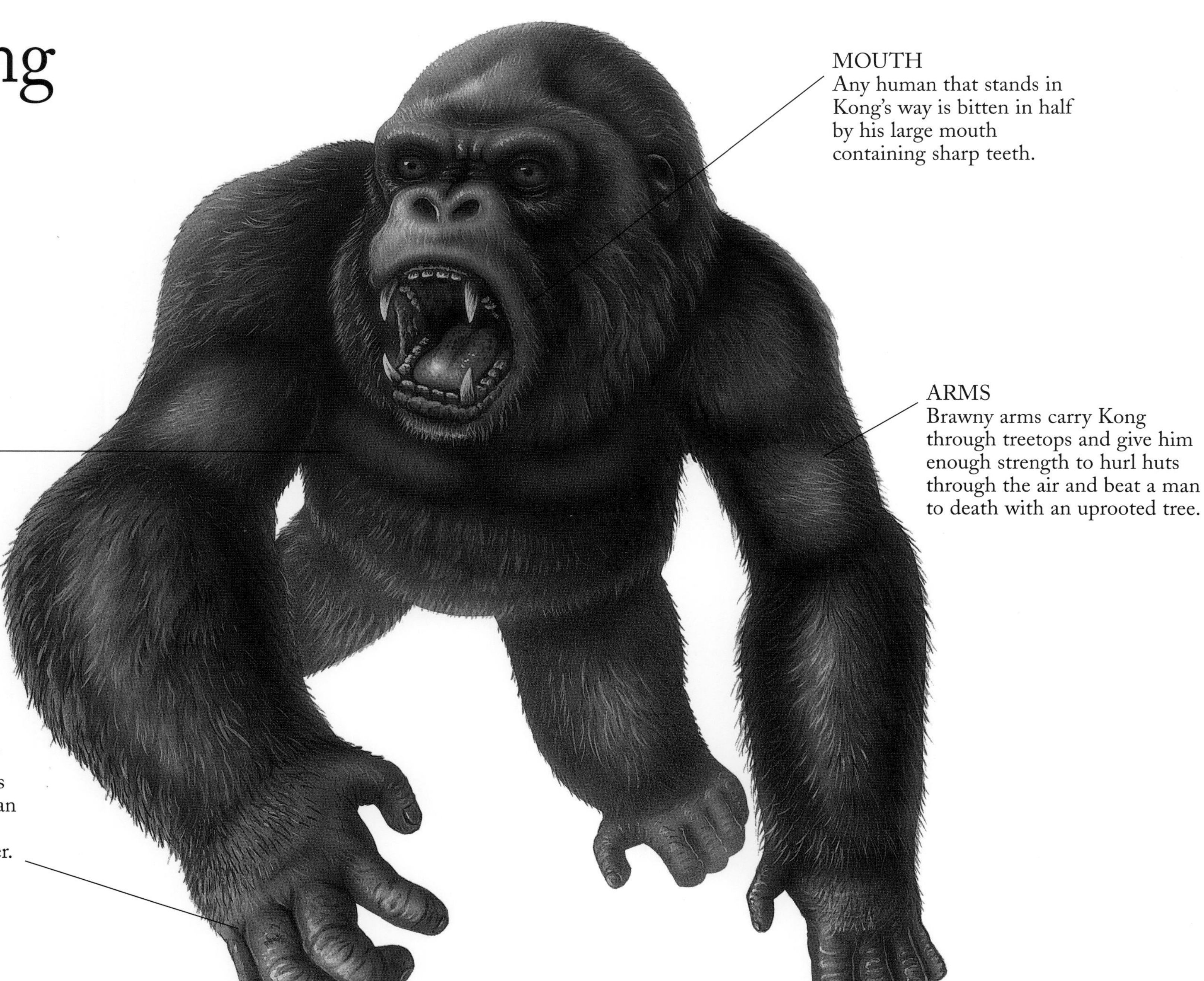

MOUTH
Any human that stands in Kong's way is bitten in half by his large mouth containing sharp teeth.

BODY
Kong's greatest weapon is his size. At 30 ft. (9 m) tall, the gorilla destroys a village and also scales the Empire State Building.

ARMS
Brawny arms carry Kong through treetops and give him enough strength to hurl huts through the air and beat a man to death with an uprooted tree.

HANDS
Massive hands are capable of flinging a train from its tracks as if it were a toy, yet Kong can also hold a woman gently in his grasp without crushing her.

A movie crew departs on a secret expedition to the Island of Skull Mountain, planning to film the ancient, monstrous wonder that lives there. The director hires a beautiful, starving actress named Ann, promising her money, adventure, and fame. When the crew reach the island, they witness a hostile tribe worshipping their jungle god, King Kong. A beautiful woman is sacrificed to the huge gorilla, as the tribe drums and chants. Ann is kidnapped and offered as a sacrifice to Kong. Tied to pillars high atop an altar, Ann can only scream helplessly at the sight of Kong. The gorilla beats his chest, bears his teeth, and snarls at Ann.

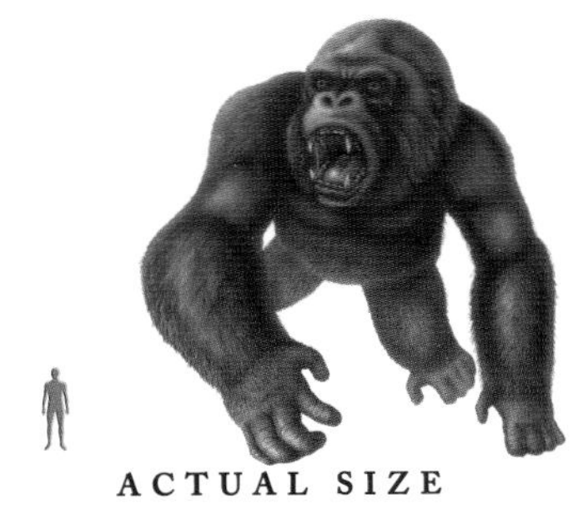

▶ KING KONG PICKS ANN UP IN ONE MIGHTY PAW and carries her off into the depths of the jungle. Numerous prehistoric creatures live within the jungle swamps of the island. Kong battles several dinosaurs to prevent them from eating Ann. The movie crew rescues Ann from Kong as the ape battles a flying pterosaur. Using a gas bomb, the crew captures Kong and transports him back to New York City, where he is put on display. Kong is chained onstage in a Broadway theater so the paying public can gawk at the "Eighth Wonder of the World."

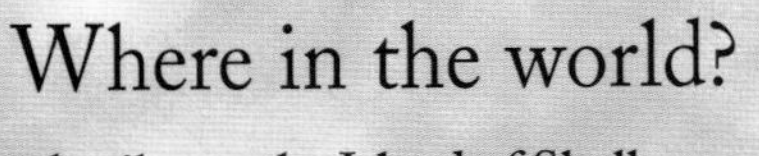

Where in the world?

A tribe on the Island of Skull Mountain in the Indian Ocean, just off the western coast of Sumatra, worships the fearsome giant, King Kong.

Did you know?

- Photographers' flashbulbs startle the chained giant, and Kong breaks his chains and escapes into the streets of New York. He destroys an elevated train before he carries Ann to the top of the Empire State Building. Airplanes open fire at Kong, and while he is able to knock one plane from the sky, the bullets are eventually too much for even the ferocious King Kong. The colossal beast falls to the street below, plummeting 102 stories to his death.

- The original 1933 version of *King Kong* was so popular that a sequel entitled *Son of Kong* was released the same year.

Luckdragon

BACK
Falkor's enormous back accommodates heroes who need to be carried through the air on important quests.

EYES
Eyes glow in the luckdragon's noble head. He is able to spot landmarks far below him on the ground even when traveling through the clouds at top speed.

JAWS
Falkor's lionlike mouth produces blue flame. The luckdragon is the only dragon known to spew blue fire. His song sounds like the golden note of a large bell.

BODY
The long, graceful body with pearl-colored scales requires no wings for soaring. The luckdragon uses levitation for flight rather than traditional dragon wings.

A dragon species in Michael Ende's novel *The Neverending Story*, the luckdragon is a wingless beast that flies by levitating. Falkor, the luckdragon in the novel, is unlike the traditional terrifying dragon. He is an optimist, believing in the power of good luck and perseverance. He tells young Atreyu that if he never gives up, good luck will find him. Even when Falkor is trapped in an enormous web stretched across Deep Chasm and struggling against a swarm of poisonous insects, he does not give up. Falkor credits Atreyu with helping him escape the web. He carries the boy on his back in search of the Southern Oracle.

ACTUAL SIZE

▶ FALKOR IS AS TALENTED AS HE IS KIND. Despite his enormous size, he is as light as a summer cloud and needs no wings to fly. He can fly while sleeping, fly on his back, and perform perfect loop-the-loops. Falkor whizzes through the mists and shreds of clouds so rapidly that Atreyu gasps for breath. When circling the night sky above the Lake of Tears, Falkor sings a song of pure joy in his bell-like voice, which is so beautiful it opens the heart of every listener.

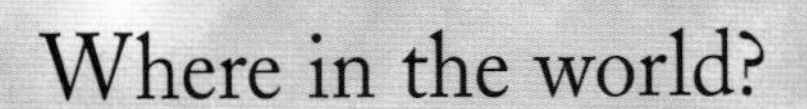

Where in the world?

Falkor the luckdragon lives in the land of Fantastica, a place where the geography is ever-changing because it is determined by wishes.

Did you know?

- Luckdragons feed on air and heat. They require no other food. Without air and heat they live only a short time.
- Viewed from the earth, a luckdragon flying overhead resembles a slow flash of lightning or a white flame.
- The rider traveling on the back of a luckdragon experiences a smooth ride despite the great speed of travel.
- As a creature of air and fire, water is the luckdragon's enemy. Water can suffocate or extinguish the flame of a luckdragon because they are always inhaling air.
- Falkor understands the language of water because all the languages of joy are closely related.

Norwegian Ridgeback

Hagrid, keeper of the keys and grounds at Hogwarts, keeps a baby Norwegian Ridgeback named Norbert as a pet in J.K. Rowling's *Harry Potter and the Sorcerer's Stone*. Hagrid wins the black dragon egg from a stranger during a card game and secretly brings it back to Hogwarts. He hatches the egg by placing it in the center of a fire. Within one week Norbert is three times his original size and smoke is issuing from his nostrils. Norbert sneezes sparks, a sign he will soon develop into a full-fledged fire-breather. The Norwegian Ridgeback can breathe fire at one to three months old, earlier than any other breed.

ACTUAL SIZE

▶ According to *Fantastic Beasts and Where to Find Them* by Newt Scamander, a required text at Hogwarts School, the Norwegian Ridgeback is extremely aggressive to its own kind, making it a rare dragon. Legend states that one carried away and devoured a baby whale off the coast of Norway in 1802. Norbert is a hazard in captivity. His tail banging against the wall rattles windows, and wounds from the bite of his poisonous fangs turn green. Hagrid must feed Norbert dead rats by the crate to satisfy his ravenous appetite.

Where in the world?

The Norwegian Ridgeback originated in the Norwegian mountains, where it eats water-dwelling creatures and singes the landscape on a regular basis. There have also been sightings at Hogwarts in England and in Romania.

Did you know?

- According to Headmaster Dumbledore, one of the 12 uses of dragon's blood is as oven cleaner.
- The Warlock's Convention of 1709 outlawed dragon breeding. It is illegal to keep a dragon as a pet in the wizarding world.
- Dragon eggs are considered Class A Non-Tradable Goods.
- Hatchlings should be fed a bucket of chicken blood and brandy mixture.
- Despite Hagrid's good intentions, Norwegian Ridgebacks are impossible to train or domesticate.
- It is especially unwise to keep a fire-breathing dragon as a pet if you live in a wooden house.

Smaug

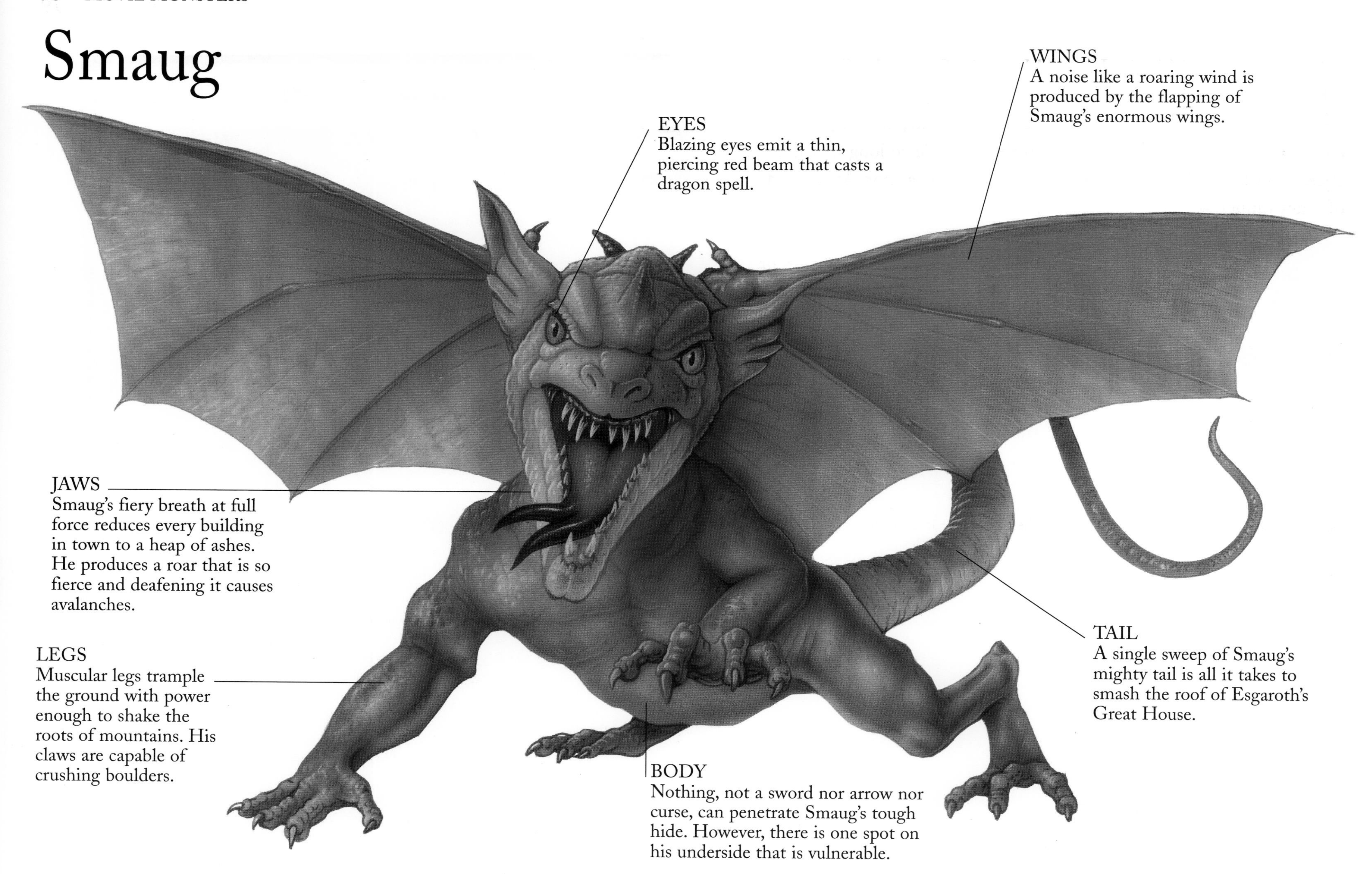
EYES
Blazing eyes emit a thin, piercing red beam that casts a dragon spell.
WINGS
A noise like a roaring wind is produced by the flapping of Smaug's enormous wings.
JAWS
Smaug's fiery breath at full force reduces every building in town to a heap of ashes. He produces a roar that is so fierce and deafening it causes avalanches.
LEGS
Muscular legs trample the ground with power enough to shake the roots of mountains. His claws are capable of crushing boulders.
TAIL
A single sweep of Smaug's mighty tail is all it takes to smash the roof of Esgaroth's Great House.
BODY
Nothing, not a sword nor arrow nor curse, can penetrate Smaug's tough hide. However, there is one spot on his underside that is vulnerable.

Isolated deep within the Lonely Mountain, Smaug the Golden sleeps atop the pile of treasure that he stole from the dwarves. Smaug makes his bed on the mass of ornaments, utensils, weapons, and gems that he hoards. He lies upon the gems for so long that they stick to his soft belly, forming a dazzling protective armor. At the end of a hot tunnel in a dungeon hall dug by dwarves, Smaug's gurgling snore can be heard. His lair gives off an eerie red glow and wisps of vapor. Although one of Smaug's drooping eyelids stays open enough to watch for thieves, Bilbo the hobbit is able to sneak in and steal a two-handled cup from the treasure hoard.

ACTUAL SIZE

▶ The discovery of this theft infuriates Smaug. He circles the sky above the mountain in a rage, bellowing and shooting flames. Later, Bilbo makes himself invisible and sneaks into the dragon's cave again. Although Smaug cannot see Bilbo, he can smell him and he mocks the invisible hobbit. Bilbo flatters the vain Smaug into rolling over onto his back. Bilbo spots an open patch in Smaug's jeweled armor. Knowledge of his weak spot is passed on to Bard the Bowman, who kills Smaug with a single, black, dwarf-made arrow.

Where in the world?

Smaug is the last of the great dragons of Middle Earth in J.R.R. Tolkien's *The Hobbit*. His lair is deep within Lonely Mountain.

Did you know?

- It is unwise to reveal one's true name to a dragon.

- Many experts believe that a dragon is able to breathe fire because it stores a mixture of gases in its body. These gases ignite upon contact with the air, producing an intense flame.

- The dragon's ability to store gases such as methane may account for its terrible stench.

- There is no record of any dragon dying of old age. All dragons in recorded history have died from accidents, disease, or battle injuries.

- Dragons have heightened senses of smell, sight, and hearing. Some breeds can see objects as far as a mile (1.6 km) away and hear sounds well out of the range of the human ear.

Werewolf

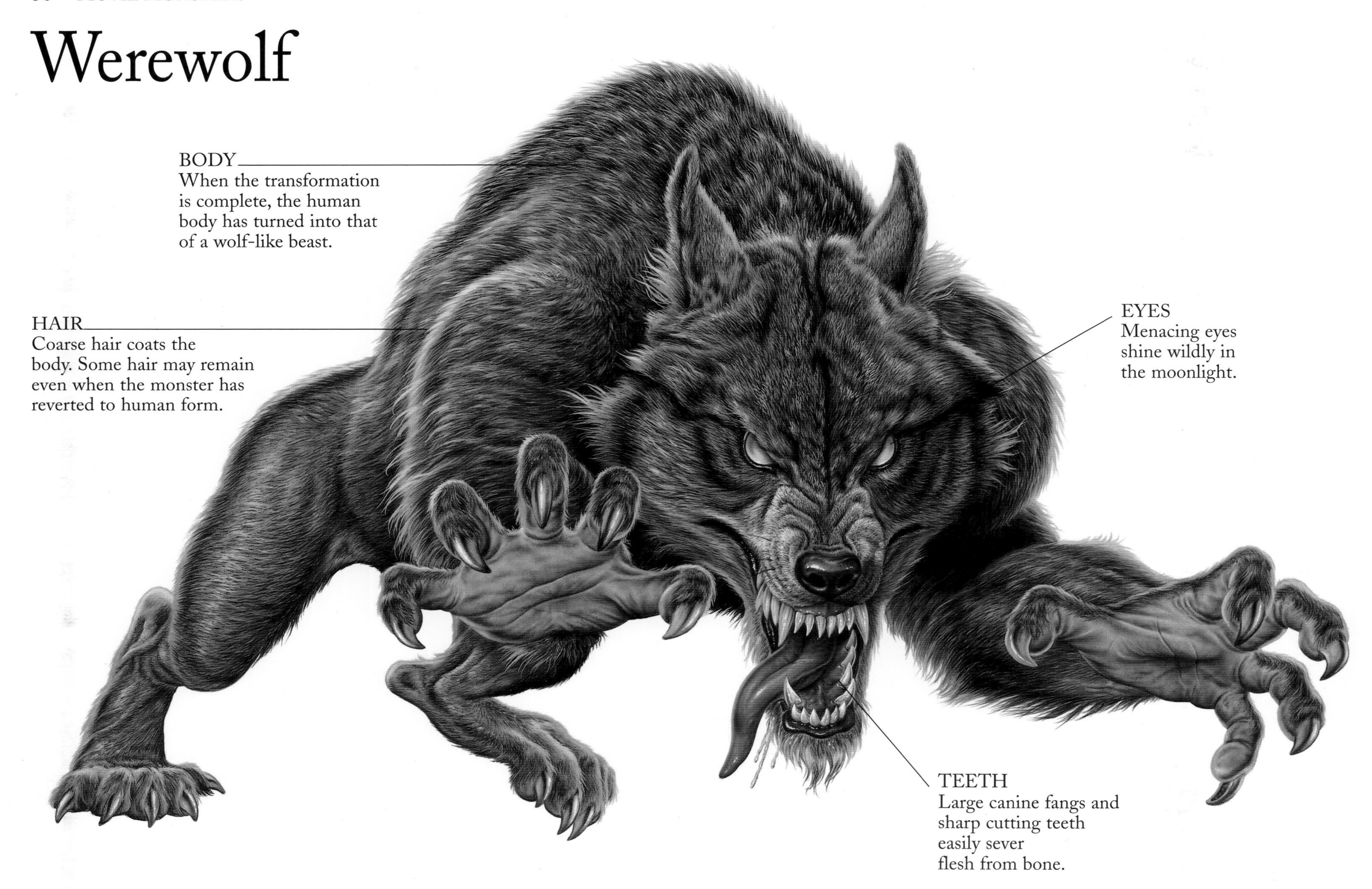
BODY
When the transformation is complete, the human body has turned into that of a wolf-like beast.
HAIR
Coarse hair coats the body. Some hair may remain even when the monster has reverted to human form.
EYES
Menacing eyes shine wildly in the moonlight.
TEETH
Large canine fangs and sharp cutting teeth easily sever flesh from bone.

An innocent-looking human by day, a werewolf changes by night into a terrifying wolfish beast. It attacks victims with vicious claws and fangs, tearing the flesh from their bones, or digs up corpses from cemeteries to satisfy its ravenous hunger for human flesh. The belief in werewolves probably grew from the fear of wolves, whose ghostly howls could be heard through the night-time forests. Belief in werewolves was particularly strong in medieval Europe, and hundreds of innocent people were horribly executed by fearful mobs. Some really believed they were werewolves and confessed to their "crimes." In fact, they were suffering from a madness known as lycanthropy.

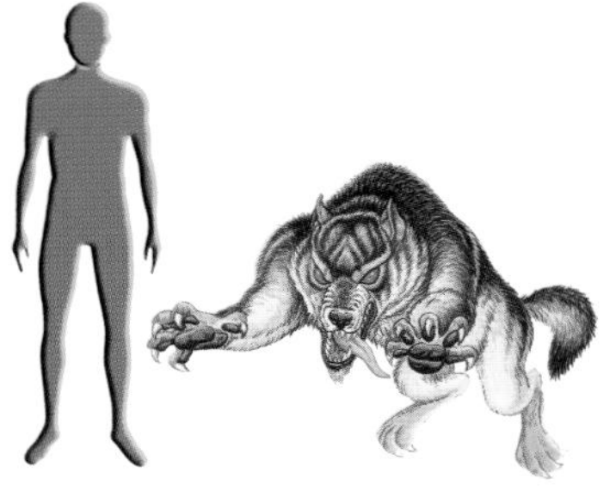

ACTUAL SIZE

▶ As THE FULL MOON RISES INTO THE SKY and moonbeams strike his body, a man is racked with sudden pain: the curse has been activated. A terrifying change takes place. His jaws stretch, his teeth enlarge into fangs, and hair breaks through his skin. He scrabbles wildly at his clothing with sharp, glinting claws. By dawn, the werewolf has turned back into a man and lies exhausted in the cemetery, blissfully unaware of his earlier crimes.

Where in the world?

Werewolf legends arose in many parts of Europe, Asia and North America inhabited by true wolves. The forests of France inspired the most stories: 30,000 cases were reported between 1520 and 1630.

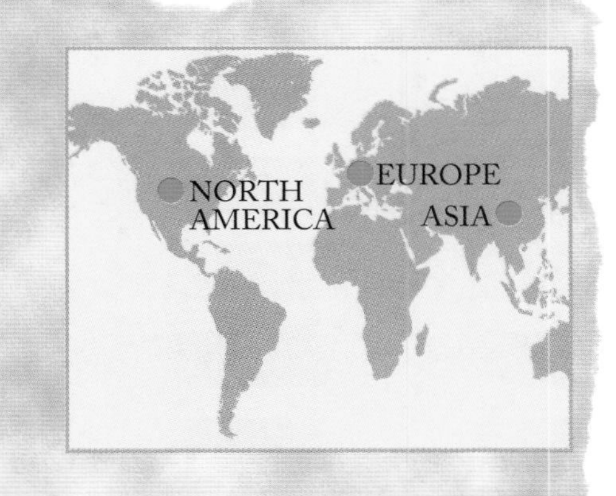

Did you know?

- In medieval Europe, people were regularly tried for being werewolves. One of the last convictions took place in 1720 in Salzburg, Austria.

- Many people believed that werewolves disguised themselves by hiding their hair inside their bodies. Suspects were often torn apart as prosecutors searched for evidence.

- Folk stories from around the world tell of people who change into tigers, leopards, hyenas and bears. Some even describe werepigs, which attack and bite passers-by.

- In European folklore, werewolves sometimes turn into vampires as they die, continuing their reign of terror.

Bigfoot

FACE
Bigfoot has a heavy brow ridge and wide, ape-like nostrils. Its eyes may shine green or yellow.

ARMS
The arms are long in proportion to the body, hanging down to the knees or even below.

SIZE
Bigfoot measures more than 3 ft. 3 in. (1m) wide, and has a stooping posture and broad, sloping shoulders. Its weight is estimated at 400 to 440 lbs. (181 to 200 kg).

HAIR
One of Bigfoot's most distinctive features is a thick covering of hair. Usually, this coat is shaggy and brown, but some people have described rust-colored, black or even glossy hair.

This terrifying, ape-like creature is said to roam in remote mountain forests, but it has eluded researchers and baffled skeptics for more than 150 years. Standing well over 6 ft. 6 in. (2 m) high, with arms down to its knees, Bigfoot can easily carry away dogs and livestock. More than 1600 instances of Bigfoot sightings or trails have been recorded in the United States and Canada since the early 19th century.

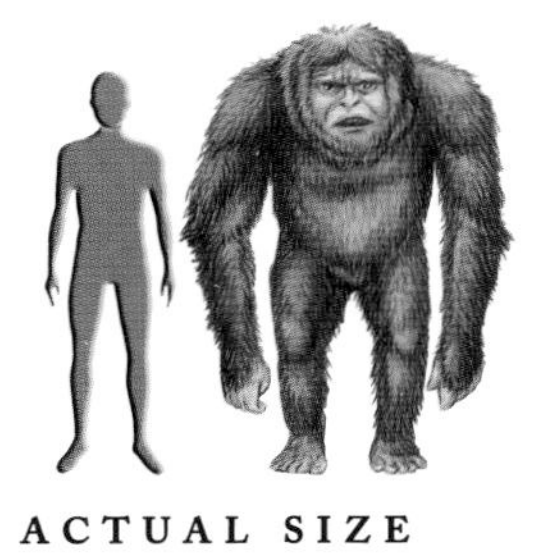

ACTUAL SIZE

▶ GIGANTOPITHECUS This giant ape was the largest primate ever to live on Earth. Fossils of two species have been found in India and China, dating from between one and nine million years ago. Scientists think the ape lived in open country, but they don't know if it walked upright.

YETI Although there have been few actual sightings of the Himalayan abominable snowman, or Yeti, many people have come across its distinctive tracks. Some who have seen the Yeti describe a creature with pale or white hair, while others report a darker coat and a pointed head.

ALMA This "wild man" of Central Asia is reputedly smaller than Bigfoot and less ape-like in build. In the late 1950s, based on his research into reported sightings, Soviet scientist Boris Porshnev suggested that these "wild men" were remnant populations of Neanderthal man.

GIGANTOPITHECUS

YETI

ALMA

Where in the world?

More than 400 reports of Bigfoot sightings come from the west coast American states of California, Oregon and Washington, and from the Canadian province of British Columbia. Other sightings have been reported from almost every part of Canada and the USA.

Did you know?

- Many people who have shot at Bigfoot from point-blank range report that the creature seems invulnerable to gunfire.
- In 1995, a sample of alleged Bigfoot hair was sent for DNA analysis to the Ohio State University. After years of testing, the results are still inconclusive.
- Hunters claim their dogs whimper and shy away from Bigfoot.

Hopkinsville Goblin

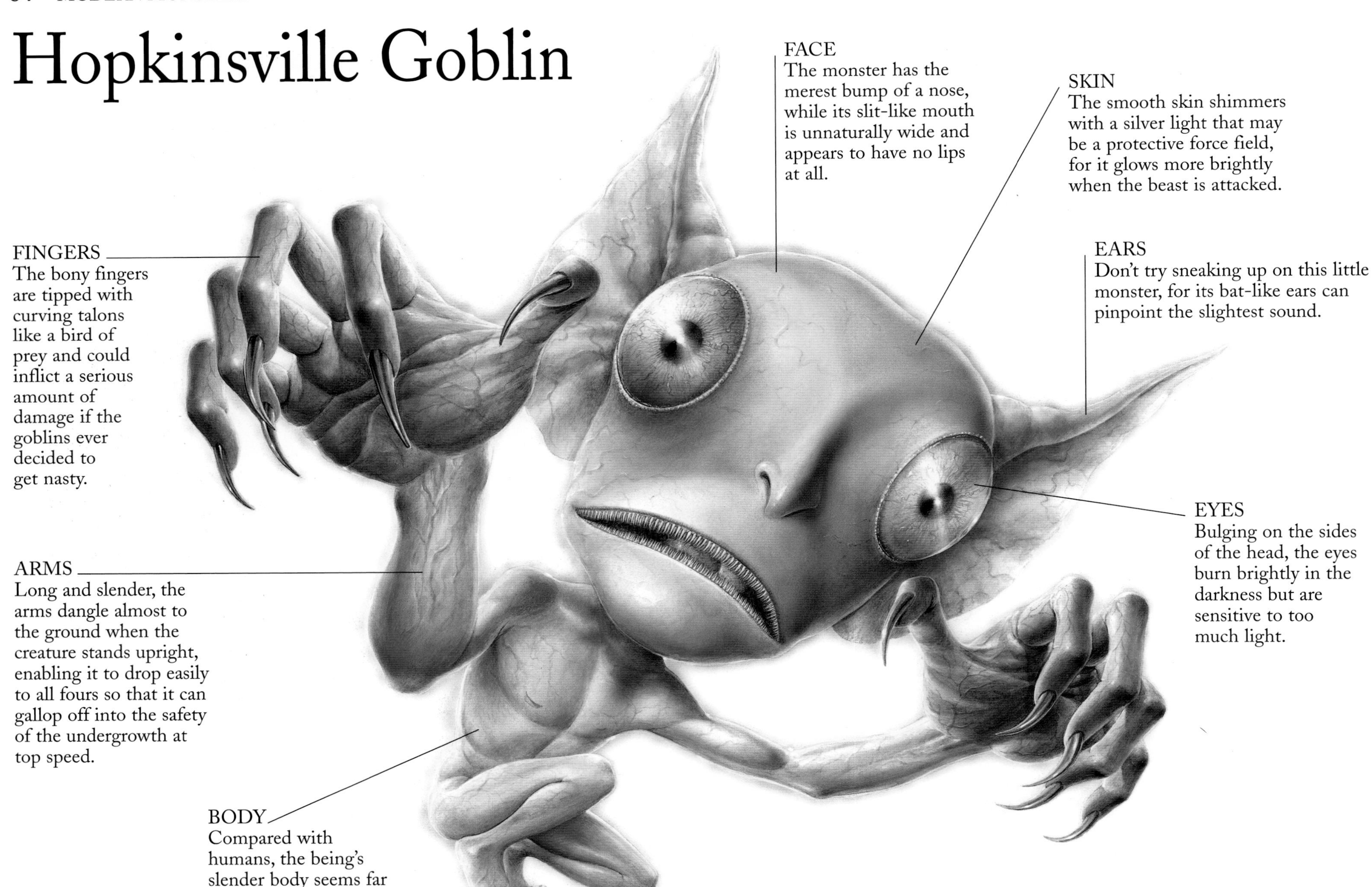

Alien or supernatural creature? No one knows the origin of the Hopkinsville Goblin, but Elmer Sutton saw one clearly enough to shoot from a tree on his South Kentucky farm. Local Cherokee Indians also had traditions of visiting night time creatures that perfectly matched Sutton's description of what he saw. The case remains a mystery, but tales of goblins have been featured in folklore since the earliest times. They are known as mischievous creatures, hiding out in underground grottoes, hollow tree trunks or hidden areas around the house, emerging after dark to scare local humans. A few goblins are malevolent in nature and have been known to get downright nasty.

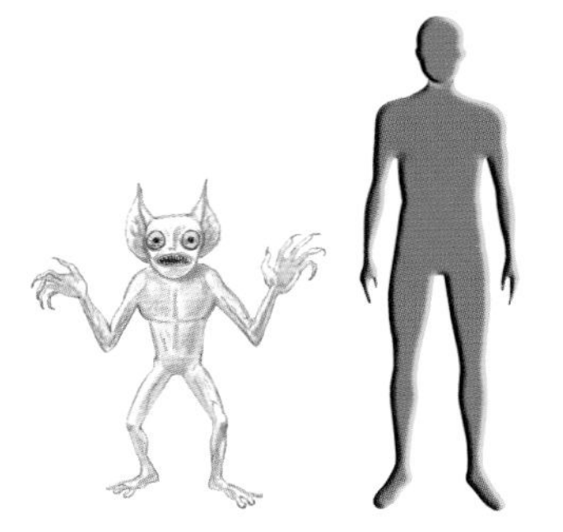

ACTUAL SIZE

▶ CREEPING OUTSIDE TO INVESTIGATE, Elmer Sutton spots a goblin sitting in a tree, and taking aim with his shotgun he blasts it from its perch. But instead of tumbling to the ground, the eerie creature recovers in mid-air and floats toward its terrified attacker before scampering off into a bush.

Where in the world?

The only documented sighting of the Hopkinsville Goblins occurred at the Sutton's farm near Kelly (sometimes known as Kelly Station), which is situated just north of the town of Hopkinsville, in southwestern Kentucky, USA.

Did you know?

- Investigators combed the area around the farm for clues, but the only signs of the encounter were stray bulletholes, although one policeman did see a faint luminous patch on the grass where one of the goblins fell.

- Local Cherokee people tell of wide-eyed beings that shunned the light and had to be chased off when one of their tribes moved to a new hunting ground. It seems that odd humanoids have appeared before.

Jersey Devil

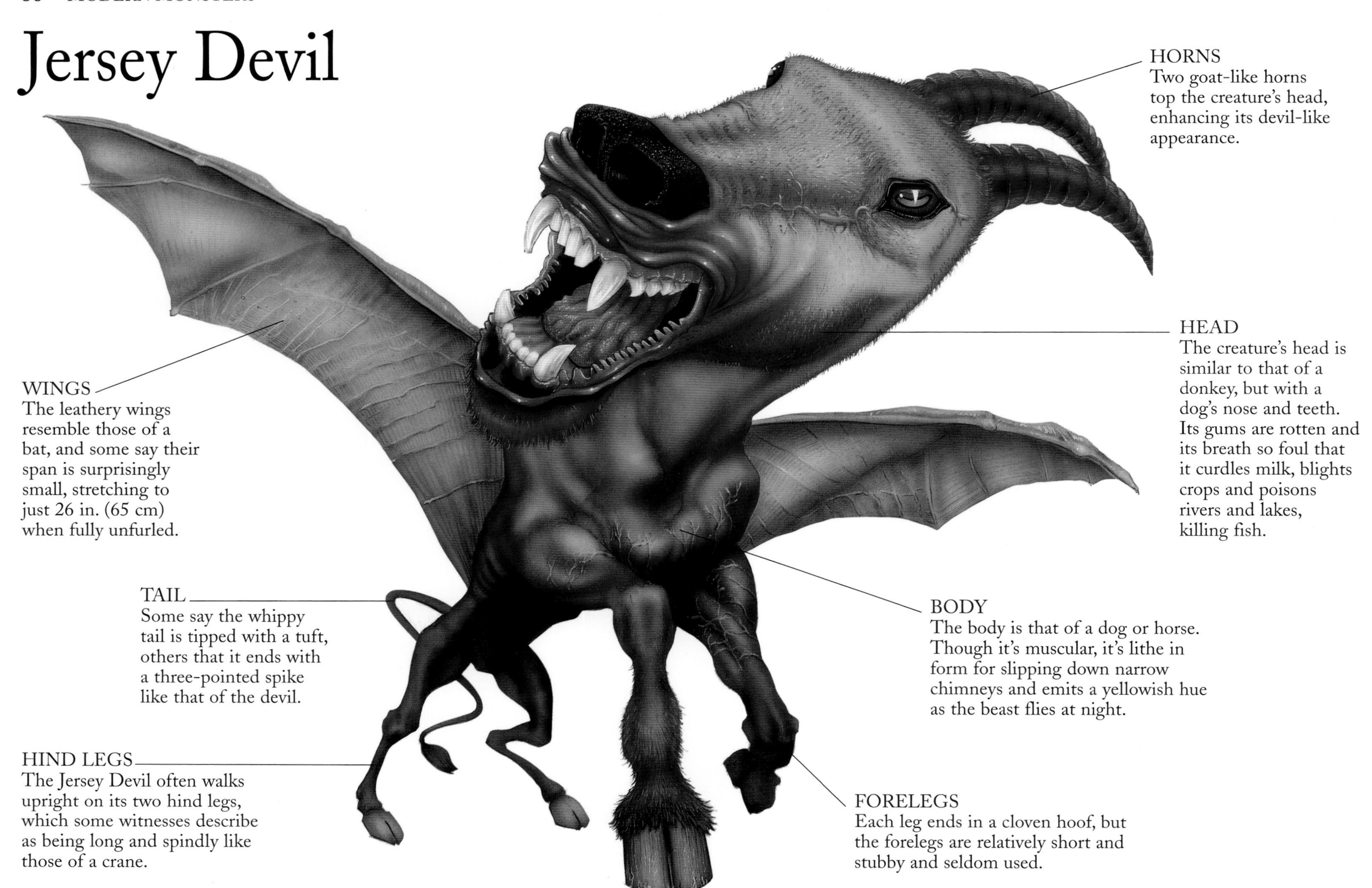

The bleak marshes of New Jersey in the USA have never welcomed people, and locals tell of strange sightings and chilling cries in the dark. According to many, something evil is out there. With bat-like wings and the head of a deformed horse, this inexplicable beast has been terrifying locals for more than 200 years. The devil emerges in the dead of night to haunt the countryside, killing wild and domestic animals and abducting small children. In January 1909, in a single week, more than 1000 people said they came face-to-face with the Jersey Devil, which appeared to householders, policemen and local officials. The accounts were all very similar, and local and national newspapers were forced to take the story seriously.

ACTUAL SIZE

▶ DRIVEN MAD BY HUNGER, the Jersey Devil leaves its dismal swampy home and flies to a nearby town, a glowing shadow in the night sky. After cruising over the rooftops, it spots a suitable chimney and dives swiftly down the soot-laden stack. The devil is unscathed by the fierce fire burning in the grate and bursts through the flames, scattering logs into the kitchen beyond. Screaming in terror at the nightmare vision, a maid watches in horror as the devil makes for the larder. She can only pray that the child upstairs remains silent—for a single cry might tempt the ravenous beast to sample fresher food…

Where in the world?

Many sightings of the Jersey Devil occur in the Pine Barrens of New Jersey: a lonely area of swamps and cedar forests covering 1698 sq miles (4400 sq km). But other reports come from all around the state, and occasionally from across the border.

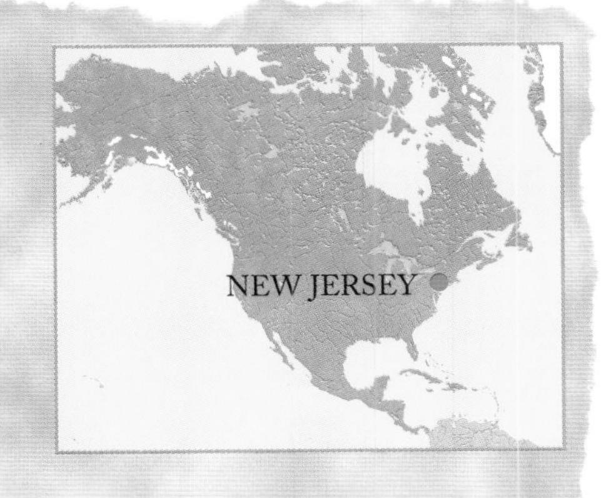

Did you know?

- In 1909, the Philadelphia Zoo offered a $10,000 reward for the capture of the devil. This has prompted several hoaxes, including a painted kangaroo with a set of false wings. The reward remains to be claimed to this day.

- When the rotting corpse of a strange, devilish creature was found in the Pine Barrens in 1957, many people took this as evidence that the Jersey Devil was dead. But since then there have been several sightings.

Loch Ness Monster

Legend has long had it that something strange lurks in the dark depths of Loch Ness—and since the 1930s, thousands of people have claimed to have seen a hump-backed, long-necked beast there. Some people claim that the "Loch Ness Monster" is actually a dinosaur whose species survives to this day in the cold Scottish waters. Other people say that the whole monster story is simply a myth invented by imaginative people. Whatever the reality, the fact remains that a number of people claim to have seen the monster. Even today the loch attracts tourists hoping to catch sight of "Nessie."

ACTUAL SIZE

▶ SOME PEOPLE BELIEVE NESSIE is a prehistoric whale called Zeuglodon (or Basilosaurus), which is thought to have died out 18 million years ago. They say it lived at sea until after the last Ice Age, then adapted to the fresh water of Loch Ness. Enormous fish called sturgeon sometimes swim up the River Ness from the sea and enter Loch Ness in search of food or mates. These fish can be several feet (meters) in length, with lines of prominent humps on their backs. They might explain the sightings of Nessie—especially when they are seen chasing salmon near the surface a long way from the shore. Loch Ness is home to brown trout, Arctic char, pike—and European eels. People believe the monster is nothing more than a large eel.

Where in the world?

Loch Ness is part of a chain of lochs, rivers and canals in the Great Glen, a geological fault that runs right across the Scottish Highlands from the North Sea to the Atlantic Ocean. The River Ness links the loch to the North Sea.

Did you know?

- There is not a single recorded sighting of Nessie before 1930.
- A handful of claimed sightings have been on land, including one of the first, on July 22, 1933. Mr. and Mrs. Spicer reported that a monster crossed the road in front of their car as they drove along the loch.
- Scientists who believe the Loch Ness Monster exists have given it a Latin name: *Nessitera rhombopteryx*.

Reptoid Alien

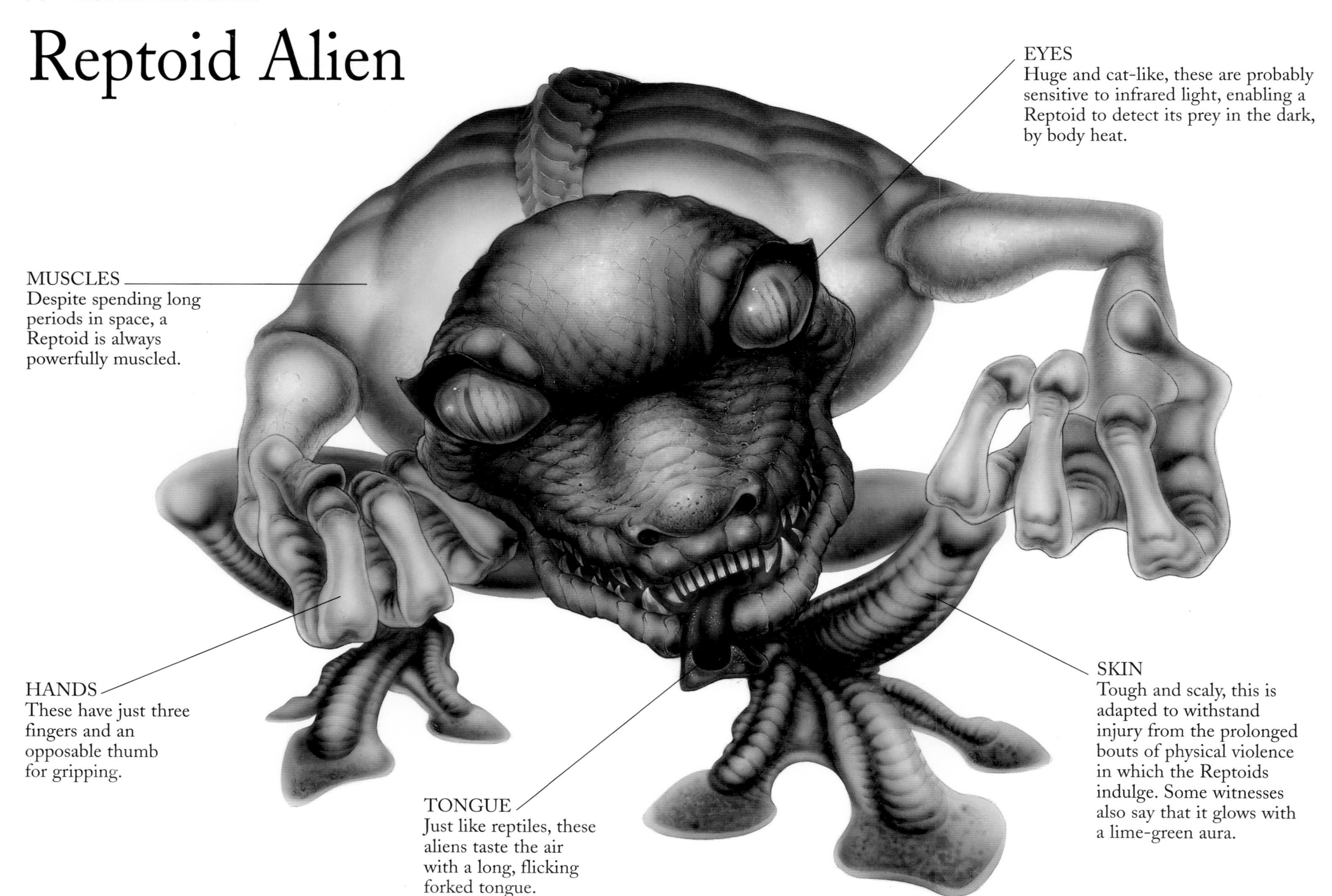

EYES
Huge and cat-like, these are probably sensitive to infrared light, enabling a Reptoid to detect its prey in the dark, by body heat.

MUSCLES
Despite spending long periods in space, a Reptoid is always powerfully muscled.

HANDS
These have just three fingers and an opposable thumb for gripping.

TONGUE
Just like reptiles, these aliens taste the air with a long, flicking forked tongue.

SKIN
Tough and scaly, this is adapted to withstand injury from the prolonged bouts of physical violence in which the Reptoids indulge. Some witnesses also say that it glows with a lime-green aura.

These scaly monsters seem to enjoy kidnapping both animals and human beings—so keep an eye on the skies. Some people claim they are aliens, while others think they are descendants of the dinosaurs. Whatever the case, they have supposedly left a trail of horribly mutilated animals across the United States. As well as being brutal and violent, the Reptoid alien is also highly intelligent. It is feared by some that one day they may take control of our planet, putting humans into slavery.

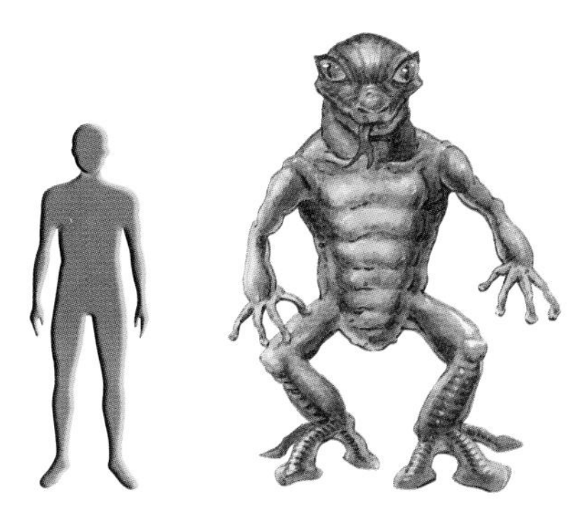
ACTUAL SIZE

▶ STEPPING OUTSIDE TO INVESTIGATE A STRANGE NOISE, a farmer is alarmed to see a spaceship hovering overhead. He becomes even more agitated when one of his cows floats up into the alien craft. Next day, he finds one of his cows drained of blood and with its eyes, tongue and innards surgically removed. But despite the evidence, the sheriff refuses to believe his story.

Where in the world?

Reports of Reptoid aliens come from around the world, but these entities are most active in remote areas of the USA. Why the Reptoids favor these regions is unknown, but it seems they wish to operate without interference from the authorities.

Did you know?

- Some experts speculate that the Reptoids consider a cow's blood and organs a delicacy; others think they use the cows as an organic resource.
- Abductees say that the Reptoids come from the Draco star system.
- Some UFOlogists claim that the Reptoids avoid arousing suspicion by transporting their invasion force safely between stars in a massive spaceship disguised as a planet.

Yeti

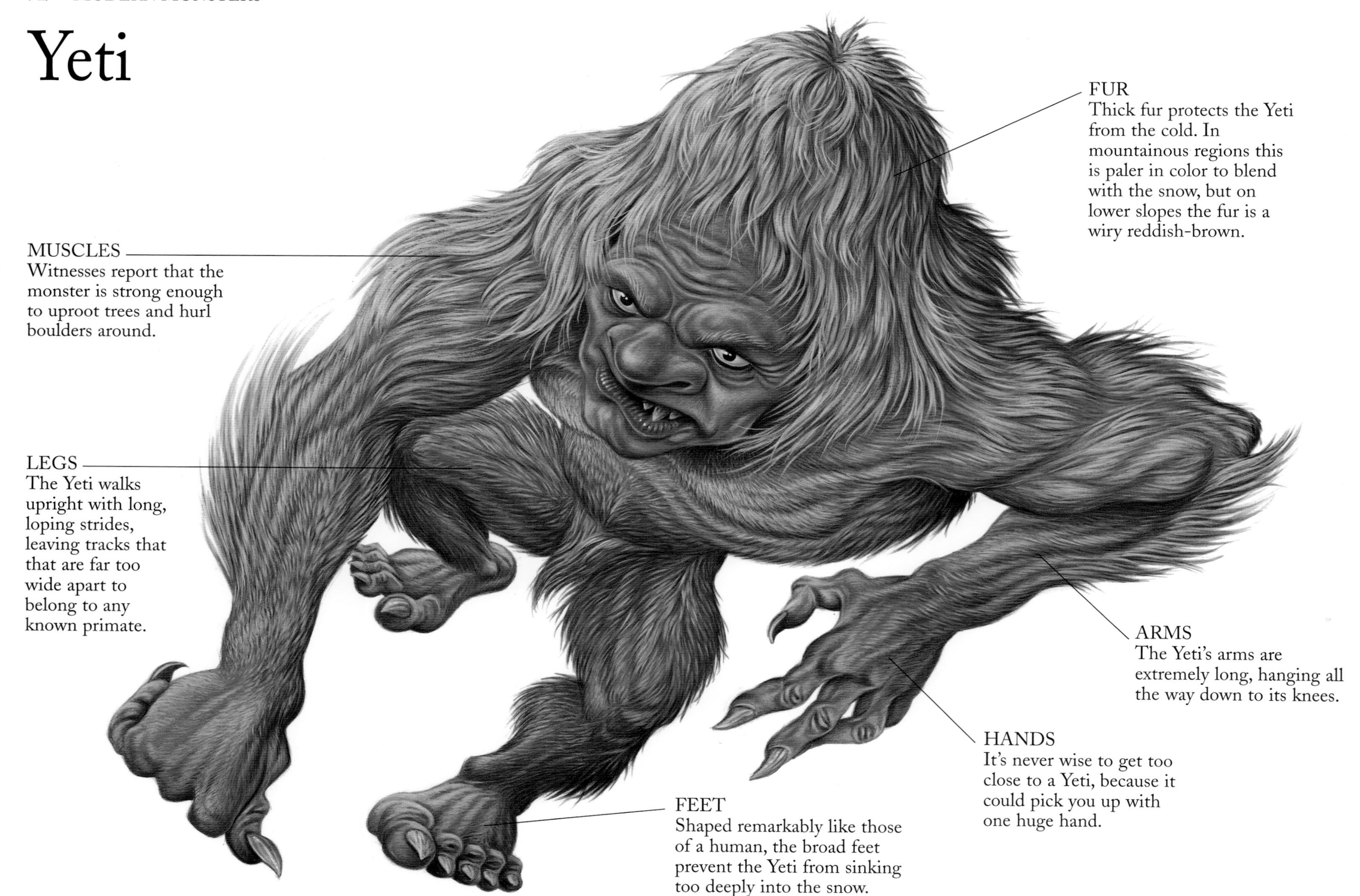
FUR
Thick fur protects the Yeti from the cold. In mountainous regions this is paler in color to blend with the snow, but on lower slopes the fur is a wiry reddish-brown.
MUSCLES
Witnesses report that the monster is strong enough to uproot trees and hurl boulders around.
LEGS
The Yeti walks upright with long, loping strides, leaving tracks that that are far too wide apart to belong to any known primate.
ARMS
The Yeti's arms are extremely long, hanging all the way down to its knees.
HANDS
It's never wise to get too close to a Yeti, because it could pick you up with one huge hand.
FEET
Shaped remarkably like those of a human, the broad feet prevent the Yeti from sinking too deeply into the snow.

Tantalizing trails of oversized footprints are often the only indication of this hairy creature's presence as it wanders across the isolated slopes of the Himalayas. Both native Sherpas and foreign explorers have glimpsed this huge, upright figure loping across the snow. The Sherpas keep a close eye on the ground, and if they spot one of the Yeti's giant footprints, they will quickly get out of the area. Yetis are territorial creatures and are said to kill and eat those who wander into their territories. Local traditions describe three different types of Yeti, the largest growing up to 15 ft. (4.5 m) tall.

ACTUAL SIZE

▶ LOST IN THE HEIGHTS OF THE HIMALAYAN MOUNTAINS, a lone mountaineer tries desperately to find his way back to civilization. But as he wanders blindly through the snow, he stumbles into the path of a huge Yeti. Howling with rage, the hairy beast rushes over and grabs the climber by the arm, incensed that a stranger has blundered into its territory. Then, striding onto a ledge, the monster dangles the unfortunate victim over a cliff with one strong arm before dropping the climber to his death on the rocks far below.

Where in the world?

The Yeti is found in the Himalayan mountain range in Asia, with most sightings occurring in Nepal, Bhutan and Tibet. But some enthusiasts have also linked the Yeti with reports of similar-looking creatures such as the North American monster, Bigfoot.

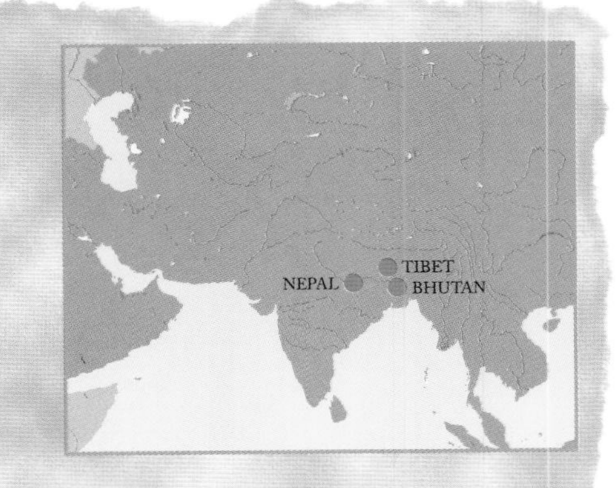

Did you know?

- In 1961, the Nepalese government officially declared that Yetis existed. It subsequently granted $10,000 licenses to any hunters dedicated and rich enough to stalk the beast through its Himalayan home.

- According to Sherpas, the Yeti is partial to a drop or two of alcohol.

- The best way to escape from a Yeti is by running downhill. Any Yeti attempting to follow will be blinded by the immense tangle of hair falling into its face and covering its eyes.

- Some people think the Yeti has transparent second eyelids, which protect its eyes during blizzards.

- The name "Yeti" is a Tibetan word meaning magical creature, but the Nepalese also know the beast as "Rakshas," the demon. The Chinese and Soviets call it the "Alma," while another Tibetan word for the beast, "Metoh-Kangmi," is often translated as the "abominable snowman."

Yowie

HEAD
The Yowie dismembers prey with its massive, downward-curving canine teeth, and in artificial light its irises reflect red—indicating the eye structure of a predator.

ARMS
The beast hurls rocks through the air and tears up small trees with its muscular arms and huge hands.

HAIR
Thick hair covers the beast's broad, fat-bellied frame, and this varies in color from reddish-brown to near black.

FEET
The Yowie can run three times as fast as a human, leaving long-toed, wide footprints in the dirt.

Huge, hairy, and elusive, the Yowie allegedly hides out in some of Australia's most inaccessible regions. It hunts by night, stalking kangaroos and other animals through the bush before ripping off their heads. The Yowie can move at amazing speed —leaping over creeks and boulders. Occasionally, it wanders close to areas of human habitation, where it watches people from dense cover, and if disturbed, the Yowie stamps its feet, beats its chest and shakes trees until they snap. Sometimes, the creature charges at intruders: screaming and growling, displaying its long canine teeth, and releasing an odor of rotting flesh and bad eggs. The beast has attacked people's vehicles, while farmers have found the Yowie feasting on slaughtered cattle.

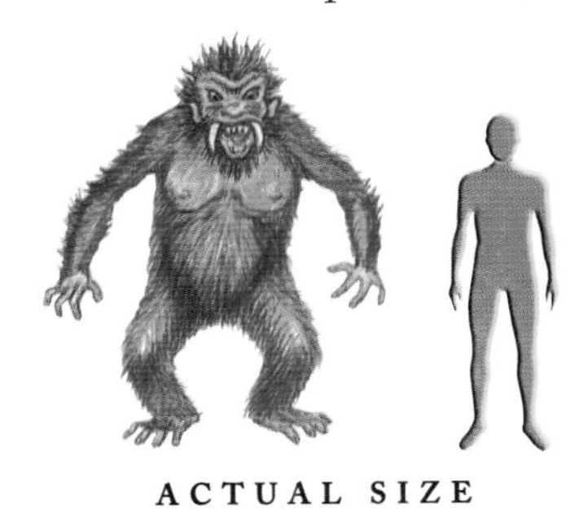

ACTUAL SIZE

▶ A COUPLE SLEEP PEACEFULLY IN THEIR NEW HOME, oblivious to the world outside. The wife's pet pooch is left to roam about the garden, and it scampers over to investigate a rustling in the bushes. Suddenly, a hulking figure looms into view, sending the dog into a frenzied fit of barking. All is calm the following morning, and after breakfast, the woman goes out to feed her pet. But she calls in vain, and when the couple search carefully, her husband finds a torn and bloodied collar. It seems the Yowie devoured the yapping terrier as a snack.

Where in the world?

In the 20th and 21st centuries, Yowie sightings have been most frequent in the eastern regions of Australia, particularly in the hills and forests of the Great Dividing Range that stretches from Queensland down to Victoria.

Did you know?

- When a team of Royal Air Force surveyors landed by helicopter on a remote mountain peak in 1971, they found fresh Yowie tracks in the mud.
- In places where the creatures' prey has become scarce, people have seen Yowies scavenging on roadsides for animals killed by passing traffic.
- Yowies are immensely strong, and one startled individual even managed to overturn a moving jeep.

Index